Vision Management

Other Books in the Corporate Management Series from Productivity Press

Yoji Akao

Hoshin Kanri: Policy Deployment for Successful TQM

Smaïl Aït-El-Hadj

Technoshifts: Meeting the Challenge of Technological Change

James A. Belohlav

Championship Management: An Action Model for High Performance

William F. Christopher

Productivity Measurement Handbook

Henry Ford

Today and Tomorrow

Will Kaydos

Measuring, Managing, and Maximizing Performance

Brian H. Maskell

Performance Measurement for World Class Manufacturing: A Model for American Companies

Michel Périgord

Achieving Total Quality Management: A Program for Action

Ross E. Robson

The Quality and Productivity Equation: American Corporate Strategies for the 1990s

Vision Management
Translating Strategy into Action

SANNO Management Development
Research Center

Publisher's Message by
Norman Bodek
President, Productivity, Inc.

Productivity Press
Cambridge, Massachusetts   Norwalk, Connecticut

Originally published as *Bijon-manejimento no susume* by Sangyō Nōritsu Daigaku Keiei Kaihatsū Kenkyūjo, Sangyō Nōritsu Daigaku Shuppanbu, © 1988.

Productivity Press, Inc.
P.O. Box 3007
Cambridge, MA 02140

Cover design by Hannus Design Associates
Printed and bound by BookCrafters
Printed in the United States of America

Library of Congress Cataloging-in-Publication Data

Bijon manejimento no susume. English.
   Vision management : translating strategy into action / Sanno Management Development Research Center.
      p.   cm.
   Translation of: Bijon manejimento no susume.
   ISBN 0-915299-80-1
   1. Strategic planning.   I. Sangyō Nōritsu Daigaku. Keiei Kaihatsu Kenkyūjo. II. Title.
HD30.28.B55   1992
658.4'012--dc20   91-20051
                                             CIP

92 93 94 10 9 8 7 6 5 4 3 2

Contents

Publisher's Message   vii
Preface   xi

1   **Develop a Vision**   1
    Barriers to Management Reforms   1
    Four Ways to Change Generally Accepted Ideas   6
    Vision Unifies an Organization   15
    How to Promote Vision Management   21

2   **Strengthening Strategy Development Skills**   29
    The Changing Concept of *Strategy*   29
    Broadening the Concept of Strategy   32
    Three Conditions for Deciding Strategy   45

3   **Creating Visionary Goals**   55
    Basic Hypotheses for Considering Management
       Objectives   55
    Building Objectives   58

4   **Thinking about Strategy from Market Perspectives**   71
    Changes in the Market Base   71
    New Marketing Strategies   78
    Importance of Strategic Thinking   82

5   **Developing Products from the Perspective
    of Social Needs**   93
    The Emergence of New Trends and New Business   93
    Expectations for New Products and New Business   99

Anticipating Needs 103
Putting Need Before Technology 105
Systematizing the Development of New Products 109
Developing Creativity Is Essential for
  Developing New Products 115
Training Development Personnel 120

6 **Activities that Bring Out Maximum Energy** **123**
Developing Business Innovation while
  Using Maximum Energy 123
What Is Maximum Energy? 126
Case Study in Use of Small Groups for
  Maximum Energy 133
Future Prospects for Small Group Activities 141

7 **Skills Map for Organizers with Vision** **149**
Two Managers 149
Requirements of a Manager 152
Using Maps to Grasp Ability Tendencies 155
Assessing Your Own Abilities 163
Types of Administrators 167
Leaders for the Coming Era 174

8 **Need for a New Perspective** **175**
Paradigm Change 176
Action-Research 176
Vision Approach 178
The Importance of Top Management 179
Innovations in the Basic Structure of Management 180

Publisher's Message

To manage for the future, scientific methods, data analysis, and systematic step-by-step methods are insufficient. According to the authors of this, our latest book for top managers, vision management also requires the ability to leap through time. Managers must project an image of the future that activates the imagination of everyone involved in achieving it and that can be recognized by everyone when it is attained as well. Controversially, the authors contend that creative managers of vision must abandon an improvement mentality that holds them bound in the past and present. They must free themselves of daily problems, all the while cultivating an ability to see present circumstances objectively and systemically — understanding the interrelationships of all the people and processes of the company at once.

Vision Management reveals a new wave of thinking from Japan. It is based on ten years of enlightened discussion among top managers of major Japanese corporations and management professors from the distinguished SANNO University in Tokyo. This compelling book lays out a framework for managers to develop and combine their creative and strategic skills. In it, vision is pinned down: readers are shown not only how to create vision but also how to translate it into clear strategic goals and effective action. Managers are challenged to have the courage to experiment, to adapt creatively to the environment, and to do so without excessive management control!

Efficiency and innovation must be balanced, the authors claim. This requires that the role of management be changed, as well as the role of employees. Qualitative, not quantitative, objectives must be emphasized, which will lead to structural reform and creative thinking. You will no longer do things as you did them before. Managers will point the way, but employees will create the means. And the result will be long-term efficiency and ongoing innovation.

Creative managers are driven by the energy of the future and are successful according to the quality of the goals they construct. Vision management then consists of high-quality goals drawn from "future energy." The authors include five steps for creating visionary goals and discuss how to recognize future trends, stating that: "Growth in the 21st century will require companies to both accept the challenges involved in changing trends and to themselves generate new trends."

Four significant contributions of *Vision Management* are: (1) how to develop a company's strategic capabilities (Chapter 3); (2) how to respond to the market and *create* an environment for future growth (Chapter 4); (3) how to recognize *and* create trends in new product development (Chapter 5); and (4) a map of 15 managerial profiles for improving creative management skills (Chapter 6).

We are very pleased to offer our management readers this "handbook in leadership training for long-term success." Along with Professor Uehara, who requests in his preface that this book generate future discussion, we hope you will be inspired to experiment with the ideas and methods contained here, and that you will let us know what you learn as you do so. The best management is a creative adventure of ongoing learning. Our wish is to enhance your learning through this and our other books in the corporate management series.

Our gratitude goes to the Research Center for Management Innovation of the Sangyo Noritsu University and to the director, Kashio Uehara, for permission to translate and publish in English the work of the Business Innovation Seminars. We also wish to thank Frank Czupryna (Daly City, California) for the excellent translation; Dorothy Lohmann and David Lennon for managing the editorial and production processes; Susan Cobb, Gayle Joyce, and Karla Tolbert for typesetting and art preparation; and Hannus Design Associates for cover design.

Norman Bodek
President

Diane Asay
Series Editor

Preface

At the Management Development Research Center of Sangyo Noritsu University, Organizational Development Seminar Meetings have been held every April since 1978. During these conferences, participants lodge together with businessmen who are actively engaged in management on the front lines of business enterprises. On the occasion of the tenth anniversary in 1988, the name was changed to Business Innovation Seminar Meetings (BI). The content and topics of these meetings have been broadened to include all areas of management innovation.

This book deals with some of the issues raised by Research Center staff personnel at those seminar meetings. Current and future management administration problems are handled as basically as possible. I wanted to help people currently engaged in management positions to continue their growth and expansion in the midst of a changing environment. There may be some places where my arguments are a bit unpolished or where opposing arguments are presented too boldly. I hope readers will give me the criticism needed for improvement. This book is the first of a series. I hope to keep developing this series in the future as I deal with theories and management administration techniques helpful to businessmen.

In the midst of all our training and consulting activities, we management administration people find that our ways of thinking do not allow us to analyze the realities we face and are not effective in helping us to deal with the work we actually do. This is true in many areas, including administration management theories and organization theories as well as marketing and product development techniques. We need new concepts and techniques.

Carrying out the research and development for implementing these new concepts and techniques should be a mission for our management training and consulting institutions.

In a management environment characterized by structural changes, several new concepts have been adopted by management administration. One of these is the concept of *strategy*. Management and business strategy have been understood for quite a long time now, but the concept of strategy has recently come to be used in all kinds of areas, including technology strategy, marketing strategy, and personnel strategy. Increasingly, staff personnel require the training of managers and assistant managers to include something about strategy. Objectives and contents for such strategy training are not always clear, but it seems to be a fact that, for the manager and assistant manager levels, there can never be enough required in regard to concepts such as management by objectives, leadership, and motivation.

Another one of these concepts is *identity*. The corporate identity (CI) boom has assumed more serious proportions in recent years. However, it has become a matter of intuitive problem consciousness for management dealing with an inward-looking identity that unifies the organization from within. That involves reestablishing the idea of management and redefining what business means. And this means recognizing the importance of restructuring domain (business sphere). How to construct a new identity is a serious problem that will decide the fate of companies. This applies to companies such as Japan Railways and Japan Airlines whose fundamental business structures were changed so radically when they were put under private management. It also applies to the steel and chemical industries, which are trying to change their business structures in the face of intensifying competition and shrinking demand. It also involves those companies trying to diversify.

Another complex concept that has emerged is that referred to as *corporate culture*. I think the concept of culture is probably very far removed from the world of corporate management, with its emphasis on rationalization and functionalism. *Paradigm* and *climate* are other examples of these new concepts. The concepts referred to here have only just begun to be used, and the technology is not yet in place to take practical advantage of what is implied by them. Although they are confusing, they are essential to the progress of management in transition. In the future they will be applied to real work situations, and there can be no doubt that after they have been applied for a few years, they will become tools of our management administration. All of these new concepts were born in the heat of fierce battles to shed some light on administration management problems that could not be understood using conventional concepts. It could even be said that they represent the very problematic situations in which management administration people find themselves.

In this book I would like to present a fresh look at the concept of *vision management*. This concept has resulted from my realization that as things are now, the effective implementation of management administration will no longer be possible using only conventional concepts such as planning, organizing, motivating, regulating, and evaluating. I fervently hope that this book will help to refine this concept even more by leading readers to debate, study, and implement it. And I hope to receive opinions and criticism from those persons in management and administrative positions who carry on the daily struggles in this field.

Kashio Uehara, Director
Management Development Research Center
Sangyo Noritsu University

1
Develop a Vision

Barriers to Management Reforms

Managers and administrators must know what kind of conditions, factors, or structures are necessary to achieve innovation within their organizations. Recently, this has become even more true in a management environment experiencing rapid changes in the midst of fierce competition. Such changes are affecting not only inexperienced managers bent on making a profit but also experienced managers seeking to rapidly expand their businesses. There is now a sense that improving today's good performance is not the same thing as guaranteeing tomorrow's good performance. Rather, survival depends on being able to change in many areas, including business, merchandise, distribution, and employee supervision. This is the condition of maintaining continual growth.

Managers Who Promote Reform — Three Types

The roles that organizations or personnel play in order to promote innovations vary from company to company, but in general three types emerge: the *do-it-my-way* type, the *get-people-involved* type, and the *consciousness-revolution* type.

The do-it-my-way type

The *do-it-my-way* type of manager or executive thinks that he must do the work of responding to changes all by himself. The employees or the organization are merely tools of his ideas and policy. This type is common among those who have founded and developed their own businesses. Such people have grasped the main points of business through experience. Thus, they approach

1

innovation by way of that experience. If their success rests on a novel technology, then they seek to bring about innovation by solving technical problems. Similarly, if they have succeeded on the basis of a unique product or distribution method, then they will innovate along those same lines. The innovations accomplished by the do-it-my-way type are quick and dynamic to the extent that the creativity of the managers or executives endures.

But while experience can be an asset to a manager or executive developing his business, it can also be a limitation when that manager seeks to bring about reform.

The get-people-involved type

The *get-people-involved* type of manager or executive thinks that the driving force behind innovation is the quality of the employees. This type is often found among managers and executives who have experienced the growth of business as supervisors. The get-people-involved type is proud of the entrepreneurial work she did as a supervisor. Her self-confidence is reinforced by her experience in coping with difficult challenges by broadening her information base and making bold decisions. Therefore, she wants current supervisors to act as she did. Her slogan is "Be entrepreneurial," "Be managerial," "Be sales-minded," or "Accept new challenges!" She believes that the driving force behind business innovation is the knowledge and skills of those in middle management. Her demands extend to all kinds of areas, including new business, new products, new technology, and extraordinary cost power.

The down side of the get-people-involved approach to innovation is that managers promoting this approach are often dissatisfied with those personnel who do not live up to their demands. That is because there is frequently a large gap between their demands and the actual situation. Business innovations cannot make progress on the strength of just one person. If subordinates do not function at the levels desired, a dilemma results. The question for managers of this type is what management style they should practice so that their subordinates will function as entrepreneurs.

The consciousness-revolution type

The *consciousness-revolution* type of manager and executives does not think that business innovation depends solely on his own supervision, nor does he think that it depends primarily on the skills of only one group of people. Rather, he looks to the larger direction of the organization itself. Moreover, he believes that the collective consciousness of an organization determines its direction. Business innovation, therefore, requires a revolution in the collective consciousness. This type of manager points to a crisis in business, characterized by sweeping changes and severe competition, as the reason for reform. The approach of the consciousness-revolution type of manager is more comprehensive than those of the do-it-my-way type and the get-people-involved type. To reform company consciousness, he institutes innovative measures in various areas, for example, changing structures and transferring personnel. He looks at internal areas as well, taking steps to improve education and hold meetings. Other tools of reform he employs are autonomous management methods and authority delegation.

Despite the comprehensive approach of this type of manager, here too things often don't work out as planned. There are still large gaps between expectations and reality.

Ideas (Paradigms) that Obstruct Reforms

All three types of managers and executives confront great obstacles to their goals. These obstacles are *paradigms*, or those mental models held in common by members of a society, group, or company. For the persons involved, these are the fundamental points of daily status quo perception, judgments, and activities. In that sense, they may be understood as *generally accepted ideas*, to use the popular term. In other words, they denote things that anyone would consider to be simply a matter of common sense.

In the business environment, generally accepted ideas can be found in three places: basic business perceptions, cultural values, and accepted daily behavior. According to Professor Kagoya of Kobe University, company paradigms are composed of mutual relationships involving basic views of the corporate world, value judgments, and behavior patterns common to members of a company.

The first generally accepted idea, the company members' basic view of the corporate world, rests on their common beliefs about what a company is, what the business of their own company is, and how the business should be managed. Examples of slogans that clearly define the objectives and scope of a business are Canon's "Hard right hand and a soft left hand," HOYA's "Light is communication," and Matsushita's "Human electronics." Other revealing slogans are Shin-Nittetsu's "Steel is the country," or Canon's "Triple spirit." These are generally accepted ideas reflecting basic views of business.

The second generally accepted idea is "climate." This can be described as the body of do's and don't's that have become tacitly understood as acceptable behavior patterns. These might be called conventional behavior patterns. Because they are conventional, they become the object of sanctions when they are violated by members of the organization. They are reinforced by pressure from the immediate environment. In that sense, survival in the organization is contingent upon observation of those conventions. They must be observed even if they are contradictory, irrational, or irritating, which indeed is often the case.

The business climate comprises customs in dealing with superiors, rules about work performance, and standard methods in deciding objectives. At some companies, a purchase costing five million dollars or more requires prior investigation, an intra-section study, and an excellent planning report. At other companies, purchases are left up to the discretion of the supervisor as long as he or she stays within budget. Administration costs are determined by the business climate. In some companies, new ways of doing things invite criticism, whereas they are accepted and even welcomed at other companies. Thus, climate even has the power to regulate creativity.

The third generally accepted idea is corporate culture. While climate reveals values that govern daily behavior, culture functions as a value to be pursued. Therefore, activities that are in compliance with corporate culture and the results of those activities are applauded. As theory, culture is revealed in the form of management concepts, behavior guidelines, company policy, and company rules. The practices of culture are revealed in accounts of heroic exploits performed by company members or through current activities.

In any case, culture stimulates people spiritually, idealistically, and intellectually. It is not surprising, therefore, that climate and culture occasionally provoke controversy. As shown in Figure 1-1, there are mutual interrelationships among basic worldview, climate, and culture. Generally accepted ideas are characterized more by irrationality, blind faith, and personal preferences than by any rational or calculating motives. That is why they are so resistant to change even if unsuited to a modern business environment. There are three specific reasons for this resistance to change.

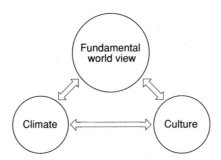

**Figure 1-1. Three Generally Accepted
Ideas in Organizations**

First, the generally accepted idea is often what led to business success in the past. So it is precisely for that reason that it sometimes becomes a firm article of faith among the company's executives.

Second, customs are established as behavior standards for people. That is why it is so hard to change just one part.

A third reason is the difficulty in getting information that is understandable in terms of hard data or rational analysis. Unsuitable matters can be shown in terms of business results or performance, but even these criteria are extremely vague and therefore open to differing interpretations. Another problem is the unease among employees caused by change. Psychologists have shown clearly that people prefer stability to change.

Some Common Barriers Faced by Managers and Executives

Generally accepted ideas pose the greatest obstacle to reform-minded managers and executives of all three types. For the do-it-my-way type, the generally accepted ideas hindering innovation are those formed on the basis of past success. In this case, the ideas and behavior customs of managers and executives have themselves become barriers. It is thus pointless to hope for innovations from subordinates. Generally accepted ideas that result from climate define the parameters of behavior and rob employees of their freedom.

In companies managed by the get-people-involved type, generally accepted ideas restrict the behavior of the organization's personnel. No matter how skilled or creative employees may be, they are still limited by the company's basic worldview and climate framework, which have been tempered by the manager's or executive's nostalgia for the climate of their youth.

The consciousness-revolution type of manager or executive is often unable to devise specific methods for instituting reform. Words and pep talks are by themselves not enough to raise company consciousness. Even when people are in general agreement that there is a crisis, they still believe that the job of dealing with that crisis belongs to managers and executives.

Four Ways to Change Generally Accepted Ideas

Introducing Change to a Conservative Business Environment

For the first time in one hundred years, the Japanese Ministry of Posts and Telecommunications is making changes in its service (product). Reforms in conventional postal service were necessitated by the development of communications techniques, the expansion of private home delivery services, and a growing nationwide network of private direct-mail home delivery. These outward changes were themselves dictated by changes in consumer needs and ways of thinking. In the face of such changes, the postal service was roused out of its sluggishness and began to reform its generally accepted ideas.

The first paradigm to be changed was the idea that mail and telegram rates should always be uniform throughout the whole country. Through product diversification — the introduction of fixed date reserved telegrams, electronic mail, and other new products — this generally accepted idea was discarded. In regard to direct mail, another reform was a system that gives discounts on the basis of weight.

Other examples of companies discarding century-old ideas are the National Railways, Japan Airlines, and the Tobacco and Salt Public Corporation — public companies that turned private.

The internationalization of business requires even larger changes in Japan's economy and society. In particular, the problem of internationalizing labor, which has been debated with special intensity recently, means changing ideas that have been generally accepted for four hundred years. Japanese society certainly liberalized its politics as it moved into the Meiji period about a hundred years ago: the so-called isolation policy was discontinued. And after the war, in 1963, Japan's economy was also liberalized after eight years of debate about opening up trade exchange. After reaching this level of economic expansion, there now seems to be a demand for liberalizing culture. Political and economic liberalization result in changing plans. But culture is more a matter of lifestyles and ways of thinking. Nevertheless, a revolution has now begun that is bringing about changes in generally accepted ideas.

Changes in the Labor Environment

A new trend in business strategy has emerged recently that markedly differs from traditional business strategy. This is the practice of mergers and acquisitions (M&A), or company buying. Formerly, the overwhelmingly accepted idea among Japanese managers was the personification of the company. Buying or selling a company was a virtual taboo. This way of thinking developed in an era when companies were seen as benefactors of society, charged with a mission to provide employment and bring Japan into the age of modernism.

Today however, Japan has become, after the United States, the greatest economic power in the world. Indeed, its per capita income in dollars now surpasses even that of the United States. As a result, traditional ways of viewing companies have also begun to change. The company-buying strategy of Dai Nippon Inkikagaku Kogyo is one of the earliest and most conspicuous examples of this entirely new way of perceiving companies.

Along with this change in perception have come changes in the labor environment. Beginning with the shortening of working hours, revisions in basic labor laws have been made. But the changes are far more comprehensive than simple revisions to the law. Taking place in an economy undergoing enormous expansion, these changes have affected ways of thinking about internationalization, management, and labor. One example of this is the enactment of legislation requiring equal employment opportunity for men and women. These laws both establish limits of application so that practical responses can be made. But the true ramifications of this legislation will be missed if only the limits of application are considered.

Labor laws enacted just after the war — so-called idea legislation — guided societal values, showing how to solve problems involving labor and labor-management relations. However, recent legislation is itself guided by changes in the worldwide labor environment. It is another example of change in generally accepted ideas; it should not be treated superficially lest mistaken countermeasures be applied.

Another factor in the new labor environment was a population that was changing in terms of both its male-to-female composition and its age composition. In a labor force full of recent high school and university graduates, the view that labor is for one's country and society has become outdated. In its place is the view that you work for yourself. This is a reality of the times, and must be recognized by managers and administrators. The structural changes that have taken place in the business environment could not have occurred had there not been changes in basic ways of thinking. Making reforms in ways of thinking about business, management policy, organizational structure, awareness of employees, and other corporate matters involves much trial and error, but this is how you find out what various changes mean and how to proceed more confidently. *Promoting reform always means that a company paradigm must be changed, even to the extent of radically affecting organizational structure.* Only then can a company accept the challenges presented by this entirely new proposition.

However, the process of trial and error always involves inefficiency. To the extent that an objective has not been decided, efficiency and interrelatedness will be lacking in any measures taken, as will purpose and planning. To minimize inefficiency, therefore, changes in generally accepted ideas and restructuring of the organization should be carried out in tandem.

Two Axes for Devising Methods of Reform

To change the structure and generally accepted ideas, managers and administrators need a clear purpose and a carefully planned strategy of action. The aim is to create a good management environment, helping the organization to grow and develop. And although the role of managers and administrators in promoting innovation is crucial, it must never be forgotten that people at other levels of the organization play a major role as well.

The standard criteria by which results of changing structures and generally accepted ideas are evaluated are hard statistics on profits, productivity, and other categories. It goes without saying that figures and statistics are considered from long-term perspectives. A second criterion to consider is the relationship between the business organization and its environment. Independent adaptability is the standard yardstick used here. This means the initial flawless implementation of policies and strategies to deal successfully with factors such as competition and change.

A third and final criterion is the capacity for continual adaptation to a changing environment. This requires both restructuring of the organization and elimination of outmoded paradigms. Replacing commonly accepted ideas is the most difficult step to take but also the most important one in promoting innovation.

In the place of old ideas, new ideas must be constructed, and with them a new climate and culture. This is not accomplished easily. On the contrary, it is painful and self-denying to reject long-held perceptions.

Practical guidance requires strict control in these three areas, but especially in the substitution of new ideas for old paradigms.

The management axis

Two perspectives, or axes, must be considered when you are working out practical methods of changing structures and generally accepted ideas. The first is the management axis. This refers to the activities through which managers and administrators control and lead individuals and groups. Specifically, there are two ways in which managers and administrators can help to change the status quo (especially that of ideas): calling attention to a crisis, and setting forth a vision. These are the two poles of the management axis. Managers engage in the former activity when, for example, they predict a crisis on the basis of current work methods or points of view. Another way is to heighten perceptions by pointing out objectives. The objectives referred to here are not simply matters of statistics. Rather, they are values that constitute a vision of the future or a situation to be achieved. A crisis can give rise to many optimistic dreams about the future. Often, however, the particulars of a crisis or the way of calling attention to it cause managers to handle it superficially.

The management axis, integrated into normal management processes, is not adequate by itself for the management of change. Its instrument is skill in getting things done, and its purpose is to control. For the people who make up the organization, this is experienced as manipulation. This is where the limits of practical methods lie.

The facts axis

Another practical methods axis should be considered in changing generally accepted ideas and structures. This is the facts axis. Facts extend beyond the scope of simple control, constituting a world in which people can recognize a situation directly as their own problem. For managers and administrators, the facts axis makes it difficult to create conditions in which employees can easily grasp the actual situation. On the facts axis, one pole represents the status quo.

Full recognition of the status quo enables managers to take measures to change existing conditions or perceptions. The other pole represents the destruction of the status quo. This so-called creative destruction allows a more factual profile to emerge and renders invalid the current way of doing things. Initially, of course, wide-ranging organizational changes bring instability as people adjust to new roles and purposes. In time, however, the people come to understand that old roles and purposes no longer make sense.

If the management axis is the vertical axis and the facts axis is the horizontal axis, a matrix can be constructed (see Figure 1-2). This matrix was devised by Rikuta, of Sangyo Noritsu University, and further developed by Uehara.

A Matrix for Changing Generally Accepted Ideas and Structures

Developing ways to handle shared problems

Quadrant 1 of the matrix lists techniques for handling shared problems. Techniques such as worksite diagnosis and feedback help workers to recognize problems and collectively devise methods for dealing with them. This leads naturally to the development of a crisis consciousness, which is reflected in expressions such as "We can't go on this way" or "We have to do something about this." Thus, people strive to clarify problems even further and to plan concrete activities designed to solve these problems. The techniques group in this sphere generates improvements from within — occasionally even radical reform.

Autonomous small group activities are a classic example of these techniques. They are an outgrowth of statements such as "Let's find the problems and solve them ourselves." The purpose of small group activities is to promote growth within the organization and a sense of achievement within the individual. At the same time, they aim to create new trends. Recently, independent group activities have been extended to higher levels of the organization, thus giving administrators and top managers an outlet for free discussion not available through conventional meetings.

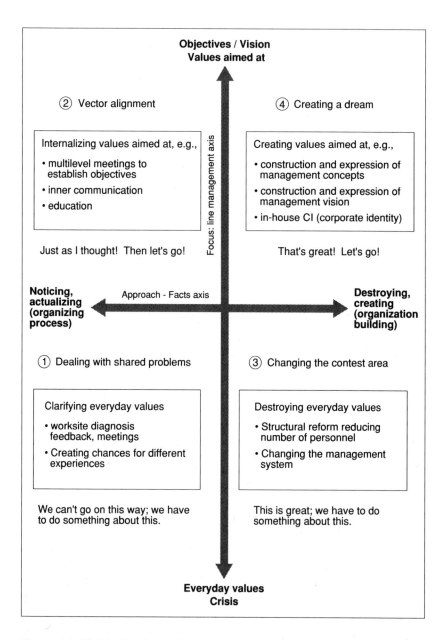

Figure 1-2. Matrix for Generally Accepted Ideas and Structures

Organized worksite diagnosis/feedback is another technique in this group. Here, company members use carefully planned methods to collect data relating to organization structure or processes (management). Feedback on the results of their analysis makes it possible to devise methods of handling shared problems and thus accelerates problem solution. This technique has been used at Matsushita Electric, Suntory, Tenmanya, Sony, and other companies. Sangyo Noritsu University, for example, uses a program known as SDP (worksite diagnosis development program).

Vector alignment

In quadrant 2 of Figure 1-2 is a group of activities that fall under the heading of vector alignment. This is a technique that creates new trends by aligning vectors while moving the status quo in the direction of objectives or vision (values or orientations that aim to change the status quo). The new values or vision are systematically established through the activities of in-house teams; they are then set forth by outstanding members of top management.

Multi-level meetings for setting objectives are a typical process consultation technique developed at Sangyo Noritsu University. While setting objectives, participants devise team activities and meetings that bring together many organizational levels. Such activities focus company objectives and mobilize employees to meet those objectives.

Another technique in this group is planned education for structural innovation. The aim is the internalization of new values and directions through education. It is hoped that as a result, work will be done independently in accordance with these new value judgments.

The groups referred to above as "dealing with shared problems" and "vector alignment" both add creative ideas to the process of organization management. The techniques involved promote innovations that are based on actual conditions. Thus, whether on a companywide or worksite scale, they are easily incorporated into normal routines. Nevertheless, because they are based on actual conditions, they can go only so far in disrupting the status quo. More far-reaching techniques are discussed in the following sections.

Changing the contest area

The techniques listed in quadrants 3 and 4 of Figure 1-2 do not proceed from the status quo. Instead, they are characterized by their ability to destroy the status quo, thereby creating opportunity for innovation. To change the contest area is to create a situation that could not have existed under the status quo. This opens the way to new trends and awakens the initiative of those close to top management.

A typical technique used to change the contest area is structural reform. There are some cases in which structural reform is accomplished through internal demands for efficiency, but in the vast majority of cases it is handled with the objective of creating trends suitable for the external environment. Examples of this approach are Suntory's sales control structure, Mitsubishi's product classification system, and Toshiba's elimination of its general affairs group. Because of these top management structural reforms, in-house personnel were required to adapt to a new system. That process raised their consciousness and shifted their orientation. Techniques that change the contest area include management reforms and major cutbacks at headquarters. An example is Tenmanya, whose main store is located in Okayama. Here, the previous number of nearly 160 employees was reduced by 30 employees, thus promoting independent activities at each worksite. Over the past few years, urban banks and other organizations have also reduced the number of their employees, providing a good example of creating new trends.

Encouraging People to Dream

In quadrant 4 of Figure 1-2 is a group of techniques designed to encourage dreams. As opposed to the techniques listed in quadrants 1 and 3, whose aim is to generate a sense of crisis, the techniques in quadrant 4 set forth future directions. They promote change by providing positive reinforcement of employees' attempts to cope with reforms. This approach is reflected in statements such as "That's a wonderful idea," or "Let's do it that way." Employed by managers, these techniques are extremely effective. They are also strategic, forming the central means by which structures and ideas may be changed. Hereafter, I refer to the use of these techniques as *vision management.*

Included in this group are techniques such as the reconstruction of management concepts like strategy. These techniques are both practical and strategic.

When people agree on the need for reform and support the methods used to bring about that end, they cheerfully cope with the self-denial involved and go on to create reform movements. It would seem safe to say that the CI (corporate identity) and other movements of the past few years are probably the first of structural reforms undertaken from this perspective. Methods within this group such as vision creation and new business development are also effective.

I have dealt with the techniques of changing structures by dividing them into the four areas defined above. These measures should not be implemented independently of each other; rather, they should be coordinated and developed as parts of a comprehensive plan.

Vision Unifies an Organization

New Tendencies in Worksite Management

Changes in the business environment naturally demand changes in the roles of managers and administrators. There are two types of change in the business world. Change in factors such as consumer needs and international competition require changes in business strategy and business structure — the creation of new business, new markets, and new products. The other type of change occurs in the labor environment and in the value judgments of employees. How companies deal with these two types of change is today a topic of strong concern.

Taking the initiative in dealing with problems

All companies, whether large or small, have objectives and policies according to which they direct their employees. Differences in their orientations are determined by management.

It is therefore essential that a system of discipline and control be based on a unified way of thinking. This is called the closed side of a company's organization. Without this, a company cannot concentrate its power and achieve its objectives. Growth and expansion are not possible on this basis alone, however. Also necessary is an organizational structure capable of adapting to change. This is because the business environment is changing internally and externally in areas that are beyond the reach of our control.

In the face of such change, a company whose closed system remains unchanged cannot continue to survive. Recent bankruptcies of previously prosperous companies is ample evidence of that. A company's ability to adjust to a changing environment by making the necessary internal changes — for example, in organization, distribution, and activities — is determined by one's own strength and the ability to accept change. The degree to which these exist results from the company's organizational structure. This is called the open side of a company.

Change in the external environment is not the only type of change requiring a response from the company. Problems also arise when top managers take on new objectives. An imbalance is thus created between the objectives and the internal closed system (administration).

Any kind of change creates turmoil in the organization. After all, people must accept destruction of the established order, shed old ways of thinking, and alter long-standing behavior patterns. A certain amount of resistance to the change is normal and should be expected. Confusion may also lead to a decline in efficiency and outbreak of problems troublesome to managers in particular. Compounding the turmoil is the top manager's own confusion.

A company's ability to overcome the initial turmoil brought on by change and continue to grow is determined by its ability to react positively — to accept the change and reconstruct its organization accordingly.

Efficiency and innovation

In a rapidly changing business environment, managers and administrators must cultivate two fundamentally different ideals: efficiency and innovation (see Figure 1-3).

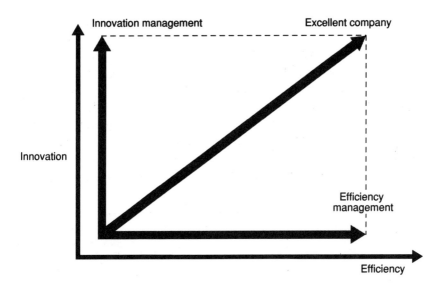

Figure 1-3. Requirements of Today's Managers and Administrators

Finely tuned management is necessary to promote efficiency. Objectives must be spelled out in terms such as percentage of cost reduction to be made or percentage of increase in yield or in sales. Moreover, the techniques to achieve those objectives should be easy to perceive. The work of each person, therefore, should be expressible in written (manual) form. Later on, it will be necessary to determine whether managers and administrators are doing their work on schedule and how to provide motivation that will increase morale. Until recently, this approach — the clarification of objectives, pursuit of improvement, and unification of values and work aims at the worksite — was sufficient for successful management of a company.

But today's managers and administrators must add another dimension to their jobs: the promotion of innovation at organization worksites. That requirement extends to all areas, including technology, marketing, work methods, and systems.

Innovation management differs from efficiency management in several respects. First, its objectives are not clear and its applicable techniques are not visible, so it is impossible to draw up manuals for it. Second, its success or failure depends precisely on the creativity and desire for challenge of managers and personnel. It cannot be implemented on the basis of efficient control and management alone. Indeed, the need for creativity is an expansion upon conventional definitions of management. Figure 1-4 shows the arrangement of management dimensions. The left side represents management that assumes the current order and ways of thinking as valid. Decisions to be made involve ways to raise efficiency or generate profits. To achieve those goals, managers need to promote work improvements, draw up manuals, increase the skills of subordinates, and develop a healthy worksite.

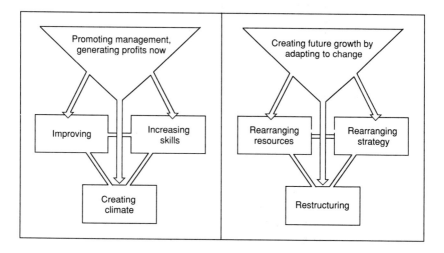

Figure 1-4. Dimensions of Management

The right side represents management that must ensure future growth and expansion by responding to changes in the environment. To achieve that goal, managers must take bold action, devising new strategies, altering the distribution of management resources, and restructuring the organization.

Develop a Vision

So far the discussion of environmental change has focused on its impact on managers and administrators. The following section treats its impact on the worksite.

Members of a diversified worksite

In the past, one of the special features of worksites in Japan was the homogeneity of their members. The same was true of the employment situation. In hiring, managers looked at where prospective employees had gone to school and whether their thinking was in line with the company's status quo. The strategy was to increase efficiency through homogeneity.

Now, however, the trend toward diversification in the worksite is conspicuous. For example, the employees themselves make up a diverse group: Along with regular employees are employees who have deferred their retirement, part-time employees, and temporary help. And of course, there are male and female employees, young and old, as well as people from many different areas of the country. Recently, even foreign employees have entered Japanese companies.

In terms of job content, if there are some persons who are doing very creative work, there are also other persons at the same worksite who have to do their jobs exactly as written in the manuals. And if there are persons whose jobs have clearly defined objectives, there are also persons whose job objectives are not clearly defined at all. Moreover, once-rigid classifications of office work, technology, technical skills, administration, and the like can no longer be clearly separated from each other.

That is why managers and administrators, while firmly rooted in this kind of diversification, must ultimately develop a type of management that concentrates its efforts on a single objective.

Bipolar culture of management

As was stated earlier, managers and administrators must work on two poles: increasing efficiency and promoting innovation. At one pole they are implementing specific methods; at the other they are providing general direction.

When considering how to increase efficiency, managers must first clarify objectives. Then they have to standardize work methods, draw up manuals, and develop standards in such a way that even recent hires can readily understand and adopt them. Checks and follow-ups during the course of a job have to be made clear and controls must be timely to deal with any deviations from standards. The objective must be a thorough elimination of waste, irrationality, and inconsistency.

Japanese managers and administrators used to take it for granted that their employees were outstanding, homogeneous in their way of thinking, and had a strong sense of identification with the company. In matters of personnel, therefore, they had no management experience. Giving general instructions when entrusting a job to someone, indicating what the expectations are, and requesting that a job be done well may not be enough. Certain situations exist that simply cannot be managed. Implementation may be impossible unless ways of doing things are completely changed.

The other pole requires managers to stimulate the kind of creativity that will promote innovations. For that purpose, managers are needed who will point out only the general direction desired. Freedom and variety in behavior and ideas are especially desirable. Such conditions are essential to the creation of long-term efficiency.

Vision unifies management organization

The coexistence of diversified workers and diversified jobs with managers whose methods and ideas move in a completely opposite direction can make for a disorganized worksite. A principle that unifies the worksite is lost. In such a situation, efforts are dispersed in all different directions and it is impossible to concentrate strength.

A new principle that unifies this kind of worksite is therefore needed. It is not a quantifiable objective, nor is it a simple matter of human relations management. And it is even less a matter of manuals or control. In order to unify diversified work and workers, it is essential to have a common vision. A common vision leads even workers with temporary involvement to feel enthusiastic about the work, while permanent workers follow this vision as if it were their own. Promoting a common vision has become even more essential for managing worksites during a period of innovation. The environment of these times requires that managers and administrators have a solid grasp of the working conditions and needs of workers and develop a vision in order to concentrate the strengths of the worksite.

How to Promote Vision Management

Management innovation means the destruction of the order that the company has itself created, together with structures, techniques, and management systems, as well as the basic ways of thinking and generally accepted ideas (paradigms) that support them. It also means reconstruction to make the corporate order compatible with a new environment. It means nothing less than carrying out activities that create the future.

A Company Is a Group Actively Engaged in Creating the Future

Corporate management is no longer engaged simply in responding to the environment. It now actively seeks to create the environment. It means setting a future course and destination for the organization and then devising means to reach that destination. Rikuta, trying to express the idea of manipulating the environment to make it conform to a desired end, coined the very apt term *environment control management.*

Managers seeking to control the environment must choose those aspirations and values that are consistent with a better future. Coping with structural reforms of an organization is a problem that involves what Weber described as "ideal organization vs. bureaucratic organization." Its starting point is problem consciousness, especially consciousness of the problem of inhumanity inherent in bureaucratic organizations. The first step is to inject the value of humanism into the organization. Later, problem consciousness develops into the realization that humanizing the organization is essential to the company's continued survival and expansion.

This results in the further realization that strategy, structural changes, and organizational reform must be handled in a unified manner. In fact, organizational expansion characterized by both soundness and adaptability to the environment is based on organizational development.

The focal point here is a management plan and vision (principles, ideas, domain, behavior standards). Rather than simply reacting to environmental changes, managers make independent choices about the course of business and then solidify them in a plan. In an uncertain environment, it is precisely this vision that secures the mobilization of energy for the achievement of organization purpose. Even for middle-level managers, the significance of this point has been increasing. Management that relies solely on systems or standards is useless. Rather, it should be assumed that creativity is the essence of management. That is because vision, not planning, is the unique unifying principle. In that sense, the principles and ideals of managers and administrators themselves are being called into question.

When you consider concrete measures on the basis of the above-mentioned assumptions, the important concepts are *the driving force* and *increasing the power to adapt*. J. P. Kotter used these terms in his book *Power and Influence: Beyond Formal Authority*.

The driving force

As shown in Figure 1-5, the first step is to decide what structural factors will become the driving force for the process of creating the future. This means deciding what parts of the status quo must be destroyed and what new standards or directions must be adopted in the work of reconstruction.

Former president Ito of the Toray Company has promoted innovation by making technical skill the driving force. Matsushita Electric is using the sales division system and in-house social systems (climate reform) as driving forces for the future. These are driven by the values set forth by management. Many software companies find their driving force in human resources. In each of these cases, the criteria by which driving forces are selected are strategies and motivations for creating the future. The driving force is created through consistent, step-by-step progress toward a long-term goal. Assuring consistency are the convictions and principles of managers and administrators, which also keep them from being entirely controlled by temporary phenomena.

Increasing the power to adapt

Increasing the power to adapt means promoting innovations by consistently increasing the overall power to adapt in each structural component. Formerly, models of adaptability for raising

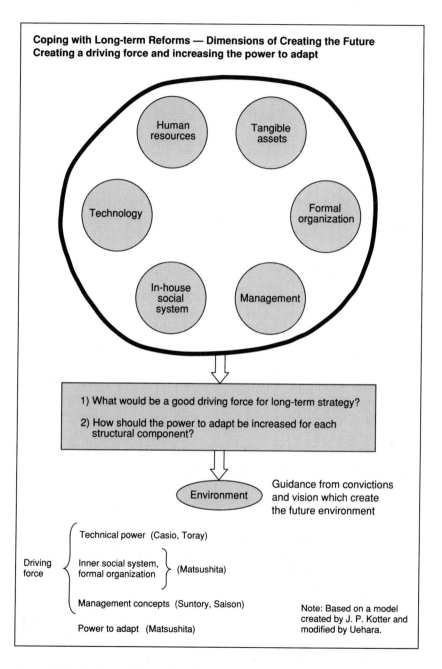

Figure 1-5. Strategy Adaptation Structure

group efficiency were based on group dynamics theory in the field of organizational structure reform. Such models then became the starting point for activating groups. They were the criteria for evaluating increases in openness, trust, mutual support, commonly shared objectives, division of roles, skill applications, conflict applications, and other aspects of organization. While using those models as his foundation, Kotter deals with the problem of adaptability more strategically by expanding the structural components of management organization (see Figure 1-6). This model changes the conventional handling of worker meetings. As a more unified model that includes both strategy and structure, it can serve as a simplified criterion until made more applicable to our work (operational).

How to Promote Vision Management

Until recently, the job of administrators was to supervise work and manage personnel. This meant that administrators spent their time controlling and checking processes such as planning, organizing, motivating, and regulating. They were expected to solve problems, make improvements, and train subordinates. They were not required to create structures that would fulfill their own intentions and objectives. Rather, they operated on the basis of conditions already established by management.

As management reset its objectives in response to the changing business environment, however, the roles and responsibilities of administrators underwent a similar dramatic change. This trend was accelerated by other factors such as the diversification of personnel. Thus, the profile of an administrator has had to be redrawn.

Until recently, the most important administrative tasks were creating structures that conformed to managerial assumptions and objectives. Today, the personal business views, management and administration principles, value judgments, and goals of administrators have become essential to the achievement of managerial objectives. Administrators must now function as the driving force behind management reform. Even for unifying and directing subordinates and worksites, the convictions and principles of administrators are

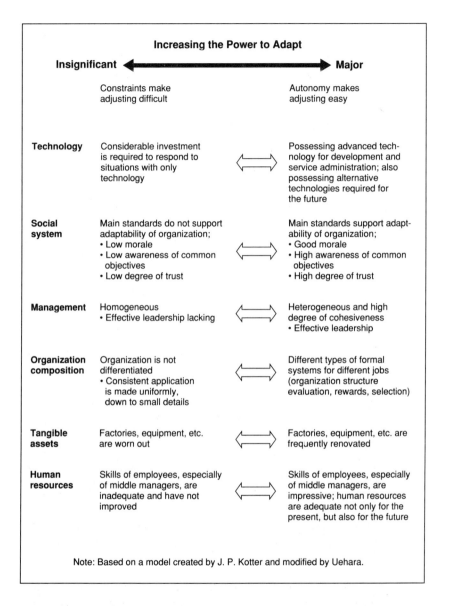

Figure 1-6. Increasing the Power to Adapt

more important than the methods and human relations techniques they use.

Vision management is management that takes into account independent management views, convictions, principles, and the value judgments of administrators as well. The profile of what administrators should be like will also have to be redrawn on the basis of vision management criteria.

Structural components of vision

Vision is nothing other than the creative thinking that administrators have themselves brought to their job — thinking based on their own convictions, worldviews, and values. They ask the following questions: What kind of place is my own worksite? What is the business orientation of my worksite? What kind of ideas must be basic to administration? Specifically, what conditions are required for the achievement of medium-range objectives? Questions like these involve the content of vision. Concrete measures must be set forth for vision as a long-range concept and as planning for medium-range objectives. Long-range vision is made up of the following components:

1. Clarification of concepts and objectives: What kind of techniques should divisions or worksites have? How and to whom should they contribute?
2. Business, role orientation: Treat the work of your own division/worksite as one job; then clarify the orientation it should have.
3. Behavior guidelines and standards: Clarify behavior standards and value criteria to be shared by members of divisions and worksites after implementing components 1 and 2.
4. Objectives: Spell out which divisions and worksites are to be involved and how far they should advance over the long term.

Normally, this sort of long-term vision is specified for a period of five to six years. Obviously, it must be consistent with the company's long-term vision. Furthermore, since this vision is always a manifestation of independent intentions and values, it is not something that changes every year. It must be something that indicates long-term directions.

Developing medium-range objectives

Normally, a company's medium-range management plans cover a period of about three years. This is true even at the division and worksite levels. These medium-range objective plans give form to vision management.

In some respects, vision management plan-making differs from conventional medium-range plan-making. According to the conventional way of thinking, strategy and planning are undertaken in the following order: establishing quantitative objectives → estimating and analyzing the environment surrounding division or worksite → identifying strategy problems → identifying individual problems → drawing up a plan of action.

These steps limit what is to be done (strategy), and make it difficult to deal effectively with problems of structural reform. And they do not deal at all with a very important point, the independence of managers and administrators themselves (what should be implemented). In other words, *why* and *what* are treated as assumptions. The only problem dealt with is *how*. This type of plan-making is inadequate in today's environment, where managers and administrators are required to initiate innovations. More creative input from managers and administrators is clearly needed. Therefore, plans should be developed according to the following steps: establishing qualitative objectives on the basis of long-term vision (specifying what circumstances or conditions should be implemented, with quantitative objectives relegated to the background) → identifying strategy problems → analyzing strategy problems → identifying problems → drawing up a plan of action. The special feature of this model is its emphasis on qualitative (as opposed to quantitative) objectives. Thus, structural reform and creative thinking are made priorities.

Management based on vision

To manage by vision, managers and administrators must first clarify their own vision, viewpoint, and objectives to the organization or worksite. Administrators who adhere strictly to the quantifiable objectives of top-level management will be incapable of vision management.

Second, they must attach importance to vision, to permeation of objectives, and to activities carried out in common. Here their tasks are to form new values, guide everyone in new directions, and determine how each person responds to the new situation. During this administration process, they make innovations that involve the division or worksite.

Third, managers and administrators must change work methods and rearrange resource distribution while trying to implement solutions to strategy problems in a timely manner. (Timing is of the utmost significance. If the timing is off, the ideas that resulted from so much effort will not be implemented.)

Finally, managers and administrators must follow through by individually examining each problem that has been identified and assigned to subordinates for the purpose of implementing vision and objectives. Managing problems is the very heart and soul of vision management.

2

Strengthening Strategy Development Skills

The Changing Concept of *Strategy*

So far, the word *strategy* has been used primarily in reference to administrators. During the last few years, however, its use has extended to managers as well. It has even become relevant to supervisors and rank-and-file employees. In fact, today you can hardly talk about management without using the word *strategy*.

In the past, strategy was often treated in manager training courses, but in many cases a strong cultural bias limited understanding of administration planning. Today, however, more utilitarian and practical considerations have taken precedence. For example, a comprehensive administration strategy will be based on the perspective of administrators, or a strategy for a particular division will be based on a comprehensive administration strategy. These kinds of changes should not be dismissed as simple trends, because they represent (1) changes in the company's situation and (2) a broadening of the concept of strategy (see Figure 2-1).

Strategy Is No Longer the Prerogative of Top Management

In essence, strategy is the action according to which the basic direction of the company is decided; its purpose is to place the company in a more profitable position within its particular business environment. In other words, it is the effort to create a situation well adapted to the external environment. For the company, that means selecting an environment and deciding how to allocate resources of the company itself. At our company, it means deciding what kind of resources and what kind of prices and markets to aim at, as well as what kind of businesses to expand. Thus, *strategy* means "strategic planning."

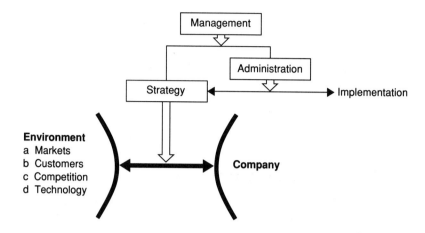

Figure 2-1. Strategy and Administration

The implementation of strategic planning requires

- a solid grasp of the general social environment involving the company
- a solid grasp of the administration environment involving the company's business in areas such as markets and competition
- a clear understanding of the company's resources and skills
- a clear understanding of company business and company organization.

Management can be defined as the implementation of strategy (and of objectives and policy) and the mobilization and concentration of energy within the organization. Various activities are carried out to achieve those goals, such as planning, organizing, controlling, and motivating.

Administration is carrying out the requirements of both strategy and management. From this perspective, strategy is the set of assumptions according to which management is carried out, while management is the action based on those assumptions.

When strategy is defined in this way, it is the prerogative of administrators. In the past managers, with the help of staff members, would carry out their management duties after being informed on strategy. Furthermore, the consulting groups that supported administration and the consulting groups that supported strategy planning could be conveniently divided into training-efficiency consulting groups supporting the improvement of management. Essentially, it seemed that administration could be divided into these kinds of strategy and management dimensions.

Today, however, the equation of administration with strategy and the growing importance of strategy make such a division inappropriate for modern administration.

Companies Are Involved in a Changing Environment

From a society of want to a society of abundance

The recent popularity of expressions such as "market maturing," "diversification of market needs," and "mass targeting versus small group targeting" testifies to the transition of Japan from a society of want to a society of abundance.

In a society of want, the basic needs of human subsistence are not satisfied. The lifestyle that most of us seek is "ordinary," which means living simply yet with human dignity. Often, the desire for the ordinary is clearly visible and is shared by many people. It is therefore relatively easy to grasp those needs. It is also relatively easy to use economic and rational standards when making judgments about things such as what kind of product service customers should receive and to what extent a product contributes to the safety, stability, and convenience of their lives.

Today, however, most people have achieved the "ordinary." Measured by conventional standards (standards applicable to a society of want), markets and needs have disappeared, as have product service development standards. In other words, market needs have become localized and diversified. So standards have become more individual, subjective, psychological, and nonrational; that is, they transcend the rational. Because of such standards, options for markets and customers have begun to increase. As a consequence, companies accustomed to operating in a society of want now find themselves needing to adapt to their new environment. This is one reason why strategy has become such an important topic.

The disappearance of models

The development of Japanese companies occurred after that of Europe and the United States. Therefore, Japan was able to learn from the experience of the industrially advanced nations (about business, product service, and technology). In that way, even if Japan failed to immediately understand environmental changes and market trends or to make the efforts required, it could still make decisions about business trends on the basis of tested methods and results.

Today, Japanese companies have taken the lead in business. With no previously collected knowledge to guide them, they have naturally become concerned with the development of strategy and with adaptation to the environment.

Sudden emergence of companies with excessive capacity

In the attempt to win out over their competitors, companies are engaged in furious efforts to make technological innovations. Consequently, the product service supply capacity throughout society has increased dramatically. That supply capacity has become an effective criterion for calculating society's demand level. Moreover, it has come to be absorbed by overseas markets, which has generated economic friction. If companies could compete and control their supply capacities, it would be possible to maintain stability and order for a short period of time. But in a competitive society, where companies have as primary goals their own continued survival and expansion, this is likely to be impossible. And in this kind of environment, it is inevitable that the topics of strategy and adaptation to the environment are significant.

Broadening the Concept of Strategy

The changing concept of strategy for management is not only the response to a new environment. Expressions such as "management equals strategy" and "attaching importance to the strategy dimensions of management" reflect a more profound change. As mentioned before, the traditional definition of strategy focuses on the relation between a company and its environment. That is, *strategy* meant "strategic planning." The point is that this so-called essential meaning of strategy has to be changed.

Analytical Strategy Theory

The theory of strategy that spawned the "essential meaning of strategy" can be generally referred to as *analytical strategy theory.* This theory typically has an analytical framework such as the experience efficiency theory (PPM and PIMS). It consists of the following elements:

1. A planned strategy (deciding management goals, selecting business areas, deciding how to allocate management resources, etc.)
2. A planning staff composed of persons who can observe management objectively, and top management decisions that are explained to the entire company
3. Analysis and estimates regarding the environment (markets, competition, etc.) that are based on an analytical grasp of company skills and characteristics; all of this is done comprehensively, objectively, scientifically, and analytically

This analytical strategy theory is based on the following three assumptions:

1. Management must adapt to trends in the management environment; that is, the company's organization and regulations must be based on economic principles. On the other hand, management cannot continuously expand the organization and regulations.
2. Management must have organizational consistency; that is, management must make efforts to adapt to the environment by using its limited resources. To use these limited resources as efficiently as possible, managers must allocate them systematically, on the basis of sound ideas and consistent policy. When management pursues its own (selfish) course, without conforming to overall company policy and ideas, the result will be lower efficiency across the board.
3. Strategy defines organization: Strategy — that is, the fundamental orientation of management — is a matter of

absolute priority; if strategy is not defined, the organization is also not defined, and personnel cannot function properly.

Doubts about the analytical strategy theory

Several doubts have emerged about this "essential meaning of strategy," or analytical strategy theory. The following are some of the more typical ones:

1. *Analytical strategy planning creates a discrepancy between strategy and the implementation of strategy.* Because strategy planning is an attempt to seize the future, it often involves getting rid of the past. To do that one must deny the status quo and discard ideas and practices that were formerly generally accepted. Such a renouncement is bound to generate turmoil and resistance to change, which prevent the implementation of strategy. Furthermore, because strategy is planned according to the logic of objective observers (who are in pursuit of economic rationalization, probability theory, and universal principles), it will meet resistance from those who implement the strategy (who represent subjectivism, specificity, and individualism). This gap between "understanding" and "doing" is what separates strategy from its implementation.

2. *The organization determines strategy.* To plan and implement strategy for structural change in a company, you must first gain an understanding of current conditions. It is impossible to perceive these conditions without first evaluating and then changing the company's basic paradigms. All the data collection and objective analysis in the world will be of no help without the changes in those basic understandings. Therefore, the nature of the organization determines strategy.

3. *Analytical strategy theory depends too heavily on analysis.* According to analytical strategy theory, the staff does the planning, relying heavily on data to win over both top managers and line workers. Therefore, most of the staff's efforts are expended on analysis. But analysis goes only so

far in enhancing understanding. Although many situations are clarified through analysis, there are also many situations for which analysis is limited as a tool for understanding. In addition, an overdependence on analysis may leave untreated those situations that are better understood through intuition and insight. Certainly many human activities cannot be fully understood until they are experienced. For example, you have to have a child to understand the meaning of parental obligation.

4. *Abstract analytical theory overlooks the contribution of subsystems to innovation.* Innovation begins from within. New trends are apt to emerge first in subsystems, which are more sensitive to impending change. Changes in the systems themselves are often the final result of those subsystem innovations. Thus, change in the management environment does not begin with changes in management policy but rather with innovations made within management subsystems.

Beyond analytical strategy theory

The limitations of the "essential meaning of strategy" theory make it clear that a new definition is needed. Such a definition would respond to the following considerations:

1. Strategy should do more than simply chart the relationship between a company and its environment. As stated earlier, strategy must be treated comprehensively, in terms of both its strategic dimensions and its management dimensions.

2. During the implementation of strategy, attention must be paid not just to the economic aspects of management but also to the psychological aspects (involving the people who implement it). In order to plan strategy that is really adapted to the environment, it is essential to integrate processes (education programs), which make it possible to change the conceptual frameworks and paradigms that managers have already internalized.

3. Management strategy should not be considered simply as strategic planning. Rather, it should be considered as *the*

development of a company's strategic capabilities. Such an approach is characterized by the following attributes:

a) respect for insights gained from the experiences of workers as well as from analysis of data
b) respect for the courage to move aggressively into the future, to accept challenges, and to experiment without preconceived ideas
c) subsystems that do not depend excessively on management (policy) but rather act independently in seeking to adapt to the environment

Internalizing Strategy Development Skills

It is useful to consider the model shown in Figure 2-2 when planning company management strategy.

A strategy that includes the psychological aspects of management

The analytical strategy theory, which has so far been regarded as mainstream, attaches importance to the economic aspects of management. This theory thus equates strategy with strategic planning itself (see Figure 2-2, right).

Even when the goal is strategic planning, it is important not to give attention only to the objective and rational aspects of management — that is, the economic side. It is also necessary to consider the subjective and psychological aspects of management — that is, the generally accepted concepts and cultural values of managers.

Often companies whose objective conditions indicate that they are unprofitable are actually succeeding. Conversely, many companies whose objective conditions indicate profitability experience problems in forging an in-house consensus. "Management," moreover, is an activity that requires you to constantly cope with matters that have little relevance to objective conditions.

Consequently, management might be defined as an activity that determines what the conditions are. Or, to look at it another way, management makes calculations by doing things that cannot be calculated.

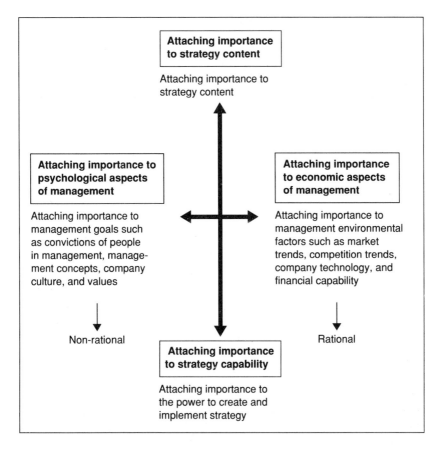

Figure 2-2. Arranging Strategy Concepts

Management is something alive. To argue about the future of management while ignoring the purpose of management itself is like creating a piece of art without contemplating your own inner world.

Developing strategy characteristics

In planning strategy, a company must also develop strategy characteristics.

Obviously, having a high-quality strategy is not a company's objective. A company's objectives are adapting to changes in the environment and bringing about the continued survival and expansion of the company. Having a high-quality strategy is nothing more than one of the conditions required for achieving those objectives. It is therefore essential to foster a company attitude that will support efforts to promptly implement strategy. Moreover, so that strategy will be in line with the new times, that attitude should incorporate a liberation from outmoded paradigms and should fully embrace the new era.

But no matter how scrupulously you plan strategy, you are still dealing with a future in which the unexpected can arise. To maintain the flexibility needed to respond to the unexpected, a company must promote the spirit to accept challenge. The development of that spirit, one of the strategy characteristics of a company, is an integral part of the strategy conceptual framework.

It has been established that analytical strategic theory fails to consider the psychological aspect of management and the strategy characteristics of the company. In the future, however, strategic planning programs will not only have to cope with the psychological aspects of management, but they will have to integrate these aspects with programs to develop a company's strategy characteristics.

When considered from this broader perspective (as it must be), management strategy is no longer the special prerogative of people in management and a few of their staff members. Rather, because it deals with the question of what management should be, it falls within the purview of all company members.

Companies that Have Superior Strategy Characteristics

The subject of company strategy characteristics can be explored in more detail through a look at some companies that have superior strategy characteristics, that is, the power to implement strategy (see Figure 2-3).

Basic attitude toward business

The way a company views and deals with its environment (markets, customers) is referred to as its basic attitude toward business (Figure 2-3, vertical axis).

1. Markets, customers 2. Products 3. Strategy 4. Business planning
5. Problem solving 6. Risk taking 7. Information, data 8. Time

**Creating the environment;
Creating markets and customers**

Systematic strategy management

1. Expansion to related markets
   and customers
2. Product groups with strategy
   consistency
3. Analysis and estimates
   consistency
4. Universality, consistency
5. Systematic analysis and
   calculation estimates for what
   strategy staff considers
   important
6. Scope of what can be interpreted
7. Internal (external), systematic -
   objective - non-personal
8. Long (interpreted as being one
   step ahead)

Creative management

1. Creating and expanding new
   markets and customers
2. New products based on new
   concepts that are more advanced
   than those of other companies
3. Concepts and missions
   consistency
4. Natural cutbacks in numbers
   of employees on the basis of
   market logic
5. Actual trial and error by persons
   involved
6. Positive and bold risk taking
7. External (internal) decisive,
   personal
8. Long (actually advancing one
   step ahead)

Basic attitude toward business

Analytical ◄──────────────────────────────────► **Intuitive**
Approach to business expansion
and innovation

Stable management

1. Maintaining existing markets
   and customers
2. Products based on existing
   concepts of higher quality
   and lower costs
3. Tendency to support conservative and stable trends
4. Planning uniformity
5. Attaches importance to
   regulations and going through
   channels
6. Maintains status quo
7. Internal, quantitative, objective,
   impersonal
8. Short

Flexible response management

1. Maintaining existing markets and
   customers; thorough preparations
   leading to expansion
2. Diverse products to respond to
   market demands
3. Ad hoc responses to market
4. Natural cutbacks in accordance
   with market logic
5. Consulting with people involved,
   political transactions
6. Relatively high risk taking
7. External, daily, subjective,
   personal
8. Short (quick response)

**Response to environment;
Response to markets and customers**

Figure 2-3. Management Styles

The question is whether to consider the environment as a stimulus or a response to the goods and services a company offers. In the first case, a company's goods and services are determined by the needs of its environment (market); in the latter case, a company's goods and services create its environment. The company that responds to the environment is preoccupied with markets and customers, trying to grasp the specific needs involved and to outdo competitors in providing a higher quality product more quickly and more cheaply. The company that creates its environment, on the other hand, scrutinizes social needs and then creates goods and services based on its own advanced technology while trying to create markets and customers. Generally speaking, retail businesses tend to become "respond-to-the-environment" types, whereas heavy industries are more often "create-the-environment" types. Ultimately, however, it is the company that decides on which type it is.

Usually, businesses whose products are determined by the environment have markets and customers that are firmly established and changes that are relatively moderate and predictable. They also have strong rapport with existing markets and customers as well as production and processing technology that is superior to that of its competitors. Businesses that create their environment, on the other hand, usually have an intuitive grasp of social trends together with a product technology that is clearly superior to that of other companies.

Approaches to expanding and reforming business

Expanding and reforming business involves selecting the best options and courses of action (Figure 2-3, horizontal axis): whether to base decisions on scientific data, analysis of the company's capacity (technology, resources, market image, etc.) and environment (markets, customers, competition, technology, etc.) or on intuitive judgments about the company as a comprehensive condensation of the past, present, and future.

The former is the "analytical approach," while the latter is the "intuitive approach." In the analytical approach, you seek an understanding of the company by analyzing the information and data at hand. Specifically, you analyze in detail each component of the area in question, study the relationships between those components, and thereby clarify the whole situation. The persuasiveness of this approach lies in its objective, logical, and rational nature. But when the subject is complex and subtle, an explanation of the parts (components) is not always an explanation of the whole. For example, a description of parts of a person's face — eyes, nose, mouth, and so on — and the relationship among the parts would still not give a clear picture of the face as a whole.

In the intuitive approach, rather than breaking down a subject into its parts (components), you perceive the subject as a whole or as a pattern, just as it is. The intuitive approach is inevitably a priori and nonverbal, and it is not easy for another person to share the perception involved. In other words, this approach lacks persuasive power. Unlike the analytical approach, however, it is highly effective in clarifying the unknown (qualitative changes, discontinuous changes, and subjects that have not yet been transformed into information and data).

Generally speaking, the conditions meriting an analytical approach are moderate changes that take place over a long period of time. The keys to an analytical approach are:

- a system for collecting and analyzing information and data
- consistent and uniform planning for transforming the results of analysis into implementation
- a system for ensuring cooperation between hands-on groups and analysis-planning staff members.

The intuitive approach requires that:

- management have a clear grasp of the problems involved and the values sought
- people work together as colleagues
- people share common perceptions about the situation in the company.

In other words, what supports the analytical approach is an organized system; what supports the intuitive approach is shared criteria for judgment (ideas).

Within these perspectives, four management styles emerge:

- Type *A*: *Stable Management Style*
- Type *B*: *Systematic Strategy Management Style*

- Type *C*: *Flexible Response Management Style*
- Type *D*: *Creative Management Style*

Attitudes toward problems

A emphasizes the sound treatment of problems.

B emphasizes the sound treatment of problems through systematic analysis in terms of objectives.

C emphasizes dealing with problems quickly, judging their relative importance in terms of external demands.

D emphasizes making practical applications in dealing with problems in order to create the situation desired.

Problem-solving styles

A does problem solving according to formal organization and rules; that is, decisions are made through proper channels and entrusted to the appropriate persons in charge. When there is any vagueness involved, importance is attached to precedent.

B does problem solving logically and systematically, with a major role played by a strategy-planning staff. It is handled through proper channels and divisions, and project teams are formed when needed.

C entrusts problem solving to the persons concerned, without adherence to formal organization and rules. Solutions are reached through consensus as a result of discussions among the persons involved.

D entrusts problem solving to the persons concerned, without adherence to formal organization and rules. Emphasis is placed on personal judgment and creative handling, while evaluation is based on performance and results.

Attitudes toward data and information

A emphasizes accumulated data that is both consistent and quantifiable.

B emphasizes accumulated data that is not only quantifiable but consistent with objectives.

C emphasizes raw data and information that cannot be quantified, although they are up to date about the front line of the worksite or business. Indicators of market needs are considered particularly important.

D emphasizes fresh data and information from outside the company even if they are vague. Information about the future is considered particularly important.

Focus of internal and external interest

A emphasizes knowledge about the strong points and skills of your own company and division. (The problem is knowing what we are capable of achieving!)

B emphasizes knowledge about the strong points and skills of your own company and division as well as about trends in the industrial world.

C emphasizes knowledge about trends in the marketplace and in the industrial world.

D emphasizes knowledge about changes in the marketplace and in society.

Leadership styles

A maintains previously acquired rights and status; it is a defensive kind of leadership.

B is leadership that emphasizes the rational and the scientific.

C is leadership that emphasizes growth.

D emphasizes leadership that encourages people to dream about the future and to believe that they are capable of fulfilling those dreams.

Attitudes toward risk

A tends to preserve the status quo, keeping risks to a minimum.

B takes risks after carefully analyzing its own and other companies' experiences.

C does not hesitate to take risks that go beyond logical and rational judgments, if the market so demands.

D encourages risk taking on the grounds that by doing so the future will be more profitable for the company.

The position of power

A proportions your authority in relation to job status.

B invests strong authority in personnel and divisions with key information, or in staff members who plan policy.

C invests authority in line divisions and worksites.

D determines authority by performance rather than by logic.

Value focus

A emphasizes speed, efficiency, and precise implementation of assigned work, that is, the percentage of activity input and output.

B is based on a logical, rational, analytical approach. Planning is carried out with finely tuned uniformity and consistency among strategy, objectives, and plans. Type *B* emphasizes activities based on such planning.

C emphasizes the sharing of information among those concerned and close identification with the company.

D accepts the challenge of risk-taking based on individual autonomy and creativity while attaching importance to the development of unique ideas.

What management style is most effective depends to a certain degree on a company's particular circumstances. For example, American-style companies tend to use the systematic strategy management style (type *B*). That is what brought about the analytical strategy theory and its practice. By contrast, many Japanese-style companies, which are supported by profits that developed later as well as by Japanese values such as group orientation and diligence, use a flexible response management style (type *C*). Moreover, desirable styles will differ depending on whether the business is about to enter a stage of maturity or a stage of decline. But a few generalizations can be made. When the environment changes more rapidly than usual, and those changes become qualitative and discontinuous, it is more effective to use an environment-creating style rather than a respond-to-the-environment style, or an intuitive approach rather than an analytical approach. In other words, it is more effective to use the *creative management style* (type *D*). This is true for the following reasons:

1. Rapid changes and qualitative-discontinuous changes promote market diversification. A management style that responds to the environment would quickly become overwhelmed in such circumstances, and in-house costs would increase.

2. Qualitative and discontinuous changes create pressure to change the business itself, leading managers to question the nature of the business. A management style that "creates" the environment can clarify intentions.

3. In the analytical approach, too much time is given to information gathering, analysis, and decision making, making it impossible for managers to keep up with rapidly occurring environment changes. By the time managers reach a conclusion, the environment has likely changed again.

4. Qualitative and discontinuous changes are changes in which the consistency between the whole and its parts (components) has been destroyed. Analysis of parts is therefore ineffective as a means by which to understand the whole. The use of insight and intuition, or creative management, is a much better strategy for that purpose. Creating the environment (markets, customers) through its own intentions and efforts, the creative management style offers the best approach to today's complex and rapidly changing environment.

Three Conditions for Deciding Strategy

The following is a summary of the main points discussed so far.

When planning strategy, managers must expand the framework of the analytical strategy theory that has traditionally been used. In particular, they need to

- introduce the psychological dimensions of management
- develop the company's strategy capacity and establish a creative management style

The following sections consider alternative strategy decision programs.

Management Concepts and Missions

The first point is to attach importance to management concepts and missions. This does not mean giving up analysis of environmental trends and company capacity but rather considering in addition to those factors the management concepts and missions that are related to management intentions. To understand the importance of these concepts and missions, consider the meaning of the word *company*.

Preserving profits

The word *company* can be loosely applied to any body established for the purpose of earning someone a living. (See Figure 2-4.) The people who enter that company presumably value the company because it enables them to eat. Therefore, a company is a way of earning a living for the people (managers and employees) who make up that company.

Strategy/objectives. For a company viewed from this perspective, preserving sales and profits is a major issue. And in order to preserve those sales and profits, you have to clarify strategy and objectives by asking questions such as: What kind of business is being operated? Who are the persons targeted, and what are they being offered? How should the horizontal and vertical expansion of business be carried out? To what extent should sales and profits be emphasized? If the conclusion is reached that preserving sales and profits is too difficult an objective, then your standard of living will automatically be lowered. Preserving and raising your standard of living requires the establishment of a strategy and objectives that are implemented in full.

Resources/capacity. Once strategy and objectives are clarified, the next requirement is the power to implement them. For that, you need resources and capacity, which involve human skills, capital, and equipment. Without resources and capacity — the direct power of a company — the implementation of strategy and objectives is impossible. This is not to say that it is all right to

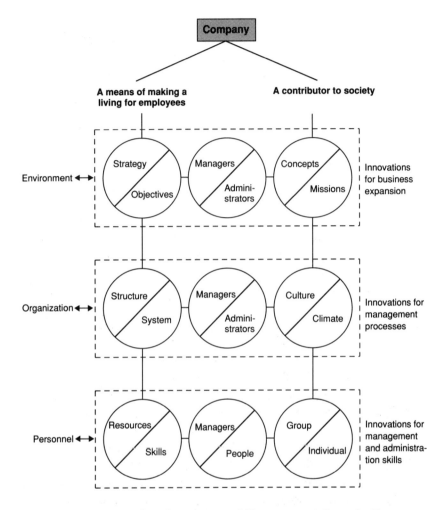

Figure 2-4. Ways to View Company and Management Organization

develop strategy and objectives without considering the present resources and capacity situation. But because companies exist in competitive environments, top priority should be given to strategy and objectives.

Resources and capacity, then, should be developed so that strategy and objectives can be implemented.

Structure/system. The next requirements are structure and system. To implement strategy and objectives, managers need to systematize processes such as the division of work required for the efficient use of resources and capacity; the building of structure required for their integration; and the motivation, control, and education of workers. It is people who carry out company activities, but people have all kinds of individual characteristics and opinions. So structures and systems are indispensable for moving them efficiently in the direction of established strategy and objectives.

Contributing to society

As was mentioned earlier, a company is a means of making a living for its members. But a company may also be defined as something that contributes to society. Even though members are working for themselves, society benefits by the goods and services they produce in this manner. The power of a company to influence society used to be limited, but companies today may have a thousand employees and the power to influence millions.

Concepts/missions. A company has responsibility not only for its own members but, as a public institution of society, for the growth and progress of society. Thus every company should ask the questions: How are we contributing to the growth and progress of society? What is meant by the term *society?* What do *progress* and *happiness* mean? It is essential for the company to establish concepts and missions to deal with such questions. The company should clarify its awareness of its position in society.

Groups/persons. Even if concepts and missions are established, nothing will come of them unless there are also soundly constituted groups and persons to implement them. In other words, while belonging to a specific company, people must also possess awareness of their responsibilities as members of society. People that have such an awareness are essential.

Culture/climate. Concepts and missions are not simple topics. They are internalized in the hearts of groups and individuals. And they are activated through the implementation of company activities, that is, through values and as regulations. In this way, culture and climate are established. Whereas structures and systems are external influences on the behavior of company members, culture and climate function as internal influences.

Implementing both aspects of a company: the role of managers and administrators

A company's function as a means of making a living may be referred to as its economic aspect, while its function as a contributor to the growth and progress of society may be referred to as its social aspect. To prosper, a company must strengthen each of these aspects. And in spite of the contradictions involved, it must implement them simultaneously.

This is where the roles of managers and administrators come in. The people in these positions must strengthen the economic and social aspects while maintaining a balance between the two.

Attaching importance to management concepts and missions for business strategy planning programs means attaching importance to concepts and missions within the models that define a company.

Why Concepts and Missions Are Important

People's changing demands

Today, because of increases in income levels, consumers demand more than the daily values of product and service, convenience and economy. Their demands have expanded to non-daily values such as entertainment and etiquette (Professor Takahiko Furuta, Aomori University). Thus, people "do not see the company as just a unit that provides for their basic needs. They see it as a unit that provides for all their needs, including those for ceremony and entertainment." This means that a company should not regard people as solely logical, rational, and economic beings (consumers) but must also view them as sensitive, individual, cultural beings (people who want a quality life).

To provide for "people who want a quality life," the company itself must be a sensitive, individual, cultural entity. If the company continues to function as a logical, rational, economic entity, it is possible that the people who want a quality life will not accept the goods and services it produces. Companies need to carefully study society's changing needs and adjust their own concepts and missions accordingly. Without such an adjustment, companies cannot expect to keep pace with changes in the environment.

Surviving in an overcrowded marketplace

The business environment today is crowded with competing companies. With so many companies clamoring to survive and expand, there has been an emphasis placed on profit that has not always contributed to the growth and progress of society. For example, resources have been wasted because of excessive packaging, excessive advertising has polluted the environment, overproduction has contributed to international friction, and intense competition has increased stress among employees.

To stand out amidst their competitors, companies are required to be unique. They usually seek to distinguish themselves through their products and services, as well as through the technology for producing those products and services. However, what really distinguishes a company's products, services, and technology is its concepts and mission, which are its answer to the question: How can our company contribute to the growth of society?

In today's information society, uniqueness in a simple product, service, or technology does not last long. On the other hand, uniqueness in a concept or mission will produce a steady stream of innovative technology, products, and services. The concepts and missions of a company — its heart and soul — are its key to longevity in the information society.

Developing strategy capacity

Three things are needed to facilitate the creative management style that offers superior strategy capacity: innovative technology capable of producing new products, companywide participation in highly individualistic concepts and values, and an autonomous and creative culture that guarantees the freedom of subsystems.

When the tendencies and landing points of environment changes remain unclear despite the collection and analysis of data, it is difficult to plan strategies. Indeed, managers often stray from priorities or fail to make decisions in such circumstances. Here again, however, the company needs to rely on its concepts and mission. Managers who pursue individual agendas during times of turmoil risk throwing the company into disorder and disunity. The result will be a decrease in overall efficiency.

In times of uncertainty, it is too time-consuming to plan strategy through discussions among divisions or among individuals. But what is worse than the loss of time is the ineffectiveness of such discussions in producing agreements unless there are shared criteria on which judgments can be based. Without these shared criteria, conclusions will be based on power relationships or political judgments.

Shared concepts and missions constitute the criteria by which judgments can be made, whether by groups or individuals. Thus, the establishment of concepts and missions is a condition for the creative management style. The keys for achieving success (KFS) in each management style are listed in Figure 2-5.

Action-Research Approach

A key requirement of a strategy decision program is the implementation of an action-research program.

The action-research approach can be described as follows: Activities are undertaken on the basis of a hypothesis or theoretical model. These activities will produce reactions, which are responses to the original hypothesis. After those reactions are interpreted, attempts are made to reconstruct the hypothesis. The reconstructed hypothesis then becomes the basis from which to carry out further experimental activities.

The aim in the action-research approach is to control the process of change in the actual situation while remaining closely involved in the actual situation.

The trouble with traditional approaches to management is their emphasis on principles of science, in the sense usually reserved for the natural sciences. The mistake is made in applying methods that are scientific in that sense of the word to a process more closely associated with the social sciences.

Company management is an extremely dynamic process. Two typical situations illustrate this point.

Suppose it is impossible to pinpoint what is causing certain results. Various factors are causing a complicated chain reaction. In

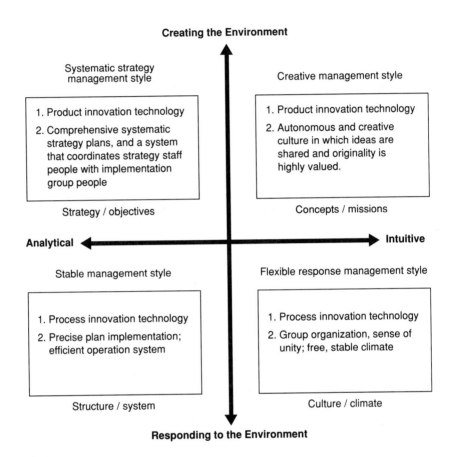

Figure 2-5. Management Styles and KFS

other words, no matter how thorough the calculations and attempts to control the situation, there are results not in accordance with plans.

Management is an imprecise science. It is impossible to make thorough interpretations of everything beforehand and exercise control. No matter how hard people may try to be omniscient and omnipotent, there will always be unexpected situations.

Just as it is impossible to interpret all situations beforehand, it is also impossible to control them through logical reasoning.

Second, in social environments such as companies, circumstances never remain fixed. Thus, any conclusions made about a certain situation themselves become points of departure. Company management is indeed a race without goals. Adherence to fixed scientific principles is impossible.

It is more effective to espouse a "60 percent" philosophy. That is, if there is a 60 percent possibility of success, the decision should be made to implement. Subsequent activities should be based on the results of (reaction to) that action. In this way, management does not aim at perfection from the beginning. Rather, it tries to create something good from mutual actions.

In other words, managers should not seek to reach conclusions about the future with information and data for understanding the present. Rather, they should use information and data about the future (bringing about some effect by doing something) so that an attitude of thinking about the future will result.

In business strategy planning programs, therefore, the action-research approach means not that business activities are determined by strategy, but that strategy emerges as a result of business activities that are themselves based on a clear goal established through efforts to clarify strategy.

This approach has several advantages. First, for every action there is a reaction. Those reactions tell something about the persons or things reacting. For example, no amount of objective analysis will tell an older person how to deal with a "me-generation" subordinate whose perspective on life differs from the older person's. Learning how to relate to others is done through interactions with other people and observation of their reactions.

When the actual situation is not clear, rather than analyze dated information or delay action, *take* action.

Second, the very act of doing something has an impact on society. During times of uncertainty and anxiety, any action taken will probably have an impact on other companies that is stronger than it would be in more stable times. Doing something therefore attracts attention and casts the doer in a central position, able to lead and create a new order.

Third, if a proposed action stands a 60 percent chance of succeeding, it should be implemented. To take action with anxieties still unresolved and with the situation still not in order is to create tension both in individuals and in organizations. Such feelings quickly make it clear what a particular situation lacks and hasten a remedy, either through acquisition of the missing elements or through mastery of activities that make up for what is lacking.

Finally, simply doing something creates confidence, both in yourself and in your organization. That confidence enables you to see what you really want to do and what really must be done.

For example, the desire to become a professional baseball player will not be realized by someone who knows nothing about baseball. Nor will it be realized by someone who simply follows the game and idolizes the great stars. Only those who get themselves dirty through hard training and who know the ecstasy of winning as well as the agony of losing will have the confidence and ability to realize that desire.

Knowing what needs to be done gives managers a strategy for action.

Of course, use of the action-research approach does not automatically guarantee success. You also need to be serious about carrying out your action and diligent in dealing with reactions. It is important for the business strategy planning programs to contain processes capable of generating seriousness and diligence. But it is also necessary to implement an action-research approach in order to generate these attributes.

A business strategy planning program, then, is something used by top-level managers to answer the questions asked earlier: What are we now? What do we want to become? What kind of contributions should we make to society? What reasons for our existence in society should we emphasize?

Having answered those questions, managers are then ready to take action using the action-research approach. This will allow them to reach firm decisions while actual work is being done.

3

Creating Visionary Goals

Basic Hypotheses for Considering Management Objectives

"An administrator walks while glancing backward, but a manager walks while looking only forward."

"The ultimate goal of administration is maintaining the smooth running of the organization. However, management is a repeating cycle of demolishing and creating, making smooth-running situations impossible."

The above hypotheses form the basic viewpoint of this chapter.

The Difference between Managers and Administrators

Consider the difference between a division head and a section chief. Both are administrators: the division head administers a division and the section chief administers a section. The division head supervises the division through the assistant director and the section chiefs. The section chief supervises the section through the subsection chiefs. The division head is the link between the assistant director/section chiefs and the board of directors. The section chief is the link between his or her own subordinates and the division head.

The division head has many more subordinates than the section chief. He or she thinks about the overall gain for the division, while the section chief is responsible to the division head for the section, and so on.

What does all this mean? It seems that division heads are nothing more than upper-level section chiefs. Their positions carry no special powers. They enjoy somewhat greater administrative latitude than section chiefs, but nothing more. However, the division head is further removed from the substantive work. In terms of what needs to be done, the role of the section chief can be considered more well-defined and dynamic.

It is not unusual for division heads to feel frustrated in their jobs, to feel that they have lost some of their dynamism. Moreover, it is difficult for them to concentrate on one goal and to produce excellent work without being rushed. Stress inevitably accumulates. If the difference in the amount of stress is the difference between a division head and a section chief, then it is hard to see why anyone would want to be a division head.

Viewed in this light, the job of division head may be unnecessary in the company organization. Each section could rely on itself to fulfill its duties. The top group of the organization could supervise these sections directly. Such a method is arguably more efficient.

But is there really no difference between division heads and section heads? Some 80 percent of the division head positions are occupied by big section chiefs. At the same time, organizations with lots of these big section chiefs have problems. In times of rapid changes they are unable to adapt. Perhaps, then, differences between the two positions do indeed exist.

In fact, the real difference between a division head and a section chief is that one does managerial work and the other does administrative work. Division heads are not middle-level administrators. If they were, then everyone else in the organization would be, too, with the exception of the chief executive officer and the rank and file.

In reality, middle-level administrative positions go as high as section chief positions and no higher. In that case, who is supervising the section chiefs? From the position of section chief and above, there should be self-supervision. Anyone incapable of self-supervision should not hold the position of section chief or higher.

Two Kinds of Energy

The division head is defined as a manager, not an administrator. That is, we can say that the difference between a division head and a section chief is the difference between a manager and an administrator. What distinguishes managers from administrators is the quality of energy they bring to their jobs.

There are two types of energy available to the leaders in an organization. The energy that leaders opt for and the importance they attach to it and its application determine the quality of their behavior and judgment.

These two types of energy may be defined as *historical energy* (energy projected from the past to the present) and *future energy* (energy projected from the future to the present). (See Figure 3-1.)

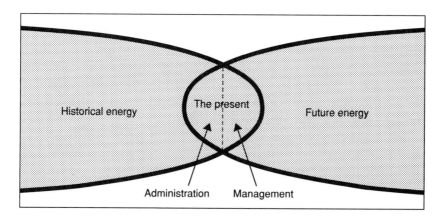

Figure 3-1. The Two Energies

Historical energy

The source of historical energy can be said to be all past phenomena. It can be defined as the energy produced by established things such as history, experience, data, climate, systems, institutions, practical wisdom, rules, and relationships. The administrative realm comes from the importance attached to these energies of the past, and one can say that administration becomes more effective by the application of historical energy.

To put it another way, administration is a pattern produced by historical energy. The administrator's approach is to justify behaviors on the basis of previous experience.

The influence of historical energy is strong. The idea of improvement is a typical application of historical energy. So is the idea of adaptation. Attempting to adapt to a changing environment certainly seems like a logical move, but it is the logic of maintenance and stability. It places the organization in the position of chasing after the environment. Development is another application of historical energy. To make conditions better than they were before, and to maintain these improvements longer is the role of the administrator.

Future energy

Future energy is power derived from the future. It is energy welling up from forgotten and distant conditions both past and present. Such energy consists of dreams, fantasies, and thoughts. It is energy created by the desire to do something in a particular way. Dreams and the like are visionary. Being unrealistic, they are considered inappropriate for the business world. Such is the limited, history-oriented, administrative concept.

The presupposition that things should be in the future the way they have been in the past is formed by an analysis of the past. In a certain sense, this is formed by historical energy.

Future energy is not confined by the past and present. It comes into existence through a gentle assertion of intentions. Managers should do their jobs by taking a hard look at past and future in a cool-headed manner while applying such energy.

If future energy is the wellspring energy of management, then giving concrete form to such energy is the process of goal construction. The true value of division heads is in their concern for the quality of such goal construction.

Building Objectives

The way you define *building objectives* depends on the way you define *objective*. There is a strong tendency to load the term with quantifiable things — for example, so many billions of yen in sales, or a rate of increase in profits of X percent over the previous year. This is because we feel more secure when setting "realistic" objectives. However, at the same time, such figures have a deadening effect. They are uninteresting.

Objectives gain meaning by being attainable. They are important as indicators of the results one seeks, and the possibility of their realization is significant. Viewing objectives as cold, hard things is the administrator's job. But that is not the way the division head should construct objectives.

Step 1: Creating Visionary Goals

The first step in objective building is the creation of visionary goals. Visionary goals map out the basic universe within which specific objectives are formed. They are an image of company organization and the world.

By describing this image clearly, a company can create objectives that are attractive as well as persuasive. Unlike slogans, visionary goals cannot be expressed in one word. They require ongoing description by the division head.

To create visionary goals, then, a company needs to satisfy the following conditions.

The logic of warp

A warp is a leap through time. The formation of visionary goals requires such a mental leap toward the future, eschewing the logic of step-by-step progress.

Projecting a management stance

The objectives set forth by the division head bear the imprint of his or her philosophy. The management stance consists of the division head's management "values," or "intention." It is that person's answer to questions such as What are our goals? What's the best way to meet those goals? Which actions do we value highly? and even What do we like and dislike?

The department manager must be wholly committed to a visionary goal. The goal's power to spur division members to action comes from the intensity of the manager's conviction. A goal for which the manager has little enthusiasm is the same as a poorly done inspirational speech or a worn-out motto.

Projecting an image of the future

Visionary goals must activate the visionary power, or imagination, of everyone working to attain those goals. A visionary goal must be such that its realization can be keenly visualized in terms of the condition each member will experience when it is achieved in terms of the benefit to be received or the impression it will make. Whatever the process of attainment might be is of no consequence. When the attainment image has been made clear for each individual, the more enchanting that image, the more intense the sense of challenge that wells up. That is important.

Visionary goals are not constrained to be "realistic." Indeed, goals that are slavishly bound to traditional concepts of reality lack the power to inspire. Similarly, those who create visionary goals have something of a free spirit. A typical example is the founder of an organization — usually a young maverick with ideas that few understand at first but that all adopt later.

Visionary goals are particularly appealing and attainable during times of uncertainty, when the future is unclear.

Giving up the status quo

Division heads must resist the temptation to set up problem solutions as visionary goals. Certainly, every organization has problems that need to be solved, and finding the solutions (eliminating the causes) of such problems is an admirable objective. But such matters are better handled by the section chief. Solutions to actual problems are not visionary goals. They do not allow the manager to project a management stance or image of the future — two conditions mentioned previously as necessary to the establishment of visionary goals. Division heads must free themselves of real problems in order to create visionary goals.

Liberation from the improvement mentality

The improvement mentality seeks to improve a certain existing arrangement or create greater growth in current capacity. Rooted in past and present circumstances, it is an example of historical energy. To create visionary goals, managers must purge themselves of historical energy, because not until the present is expelled from their thoughts can they leap (warp) into the future.

Thus, an orientation toward improvement is an impediment in the creation of visionary goals.

Step 2: Getting a Clear Understanding of Present Conditions

The second step in objective building by the division head is to get a clear understanding of present conditions. This may seem surprising in view of the previous emphasis. However, there are reasons why this step is important.

As was mentioned, while they are formulating visionary goals, division heads should ignore the present. However, once the visionary goal has been created, they must immediately return to the present. This leap from the future back to the present might be called "reverse warp."

The reverse warp may be the most difficult step in the process of goal building. The return to data that was deliberately rejected in the previous step requires a fairly tough-minded outlook.

Grasping the present must done in a cool-headed, logical way. The division head must thoroughly understand the division as it actually is. What are the conditions, then, for grasping the present?

Grasping the structure of facts

An understanding of the situation is not gained through analysis of its separate parts. Managers must take a macroview to grasp these diverse phenomena as items linked together. They must study the mutual relationships between the phenomena, and the quality and strengths of those relationships.

Grasping the present means penetrating the underpinnings of observable data. One's focus should be not on the observable data themselves but on the background to those data, the phenomena that produce and structure them (see Figure 3-2).

Facts and events such as sales for a certain period and the relationship between division head A and section chief B are significant not for their own sakes but as outward manifestations of a deeper truth. To grasp this deeper reality, managers need not only

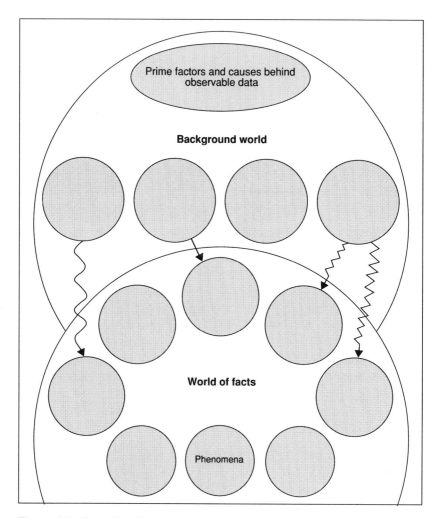

Figure 3-2. Grasping the Present

to collect facts as data but also to understand why those facts exist. Only then will they understand the present.

Resources disposition

People tend to see the present in an emotional way. This tendency creates the danger that managers will bring personal viewpoints to their interpretation of data and their underlying factors.

Division heads may be particularly vulnerable to this subjectivism, since the strong sense of self that perhaps propelled them to their positions can in fact be a liability when objectivity is required.

To grasp the background world in a functional manner, managers must know in what sort of conditions the resources for causality are arranged. They must understand the arrangement of the elements involved — people, things, money, and information — and the relationships among them.

For example, to understand a fall in the rate of profit, they must understand which people with what capabilities are serving what roles with what authority. They also must know about available equipment and machinery, how information flows, the procedures for implementing instructions, and the values and operational standards that influence workers. Managers need to approach these questions coolly and logically; they must also direct their attention equally toward all aspects.

Step 3: Recognizing Gaps

Once the present has been grasped, the next step is to recognize the gaps (see Figure 3-3).

Gaps are the "difference" between the visionary goals and the background world. Managers need to recognize the difference between visionary goals (set through a warp into the future) and the background world (grasped through a reverse warp to the present).

Once they recognize this difference, they must assume a standpoint from which to observe the gaps (see Figure 3-4). It might sound sensible to say that managers should assume a middle position between both sides. However, from this position it would be difficult to see gaps that were too big or too varied; conversely, a large gap could overwhelm the view from a stance midway between visionary goals and the background world.

What if the gaps were viewed from the background world side? The facts would be too clear and too richly colored. The visionary goals would be totally hidden by the brilliant coloring of the background. The only thing to be seen would be "obstacles." As a result, managers might succumb to the temptation to focus on those prime factors and causes with the richest coloring.

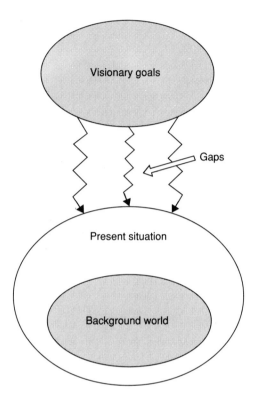

Figure 3-3. Recognizing the Gaps

But what if the gaps were viewed from the visionary goal side? Visionary goals are three-dimensional images infused with light. While it is a bright light, it is also a clear one, and through it you can see into the background world. A path of light of several beams linking the visionary goals and the background world ought to become visible. Of these, the most brilliant are the strategic goals. The gaps must be seen through the visionary goals.

Step 4: Creating Strategy Objectives

Strategy objectives are means for bringing the present in line with visionary goals. When strategy objectives are attained, the gaps between the background world and the visionary goals are dissolved (see Figure 3-5). How then are strategy objectives established?

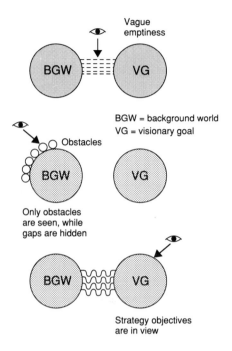

Figure 3-4. Is the VG Visible?

Importance of efficiency

In setting strategy objectives, efficiency is important. Efficiency means resolving the problems of those strategy objectives, and dissolving the gaps between visionary goals and the background world. It is easy to attain strategy objectives if your standards in setting them are low. But recognition of whether the gaps have been eliminated through the attainment of strategic objectives requires concentrated thinking.

Considering possibilities

Once you have decided on strategy objectives, you must think about possibilities. Specifically, you need to consider two kinds of possibilities.

One type is the *possibility of attainment*. This is the probability that the strategic goals are attainable. If they are not — that is,

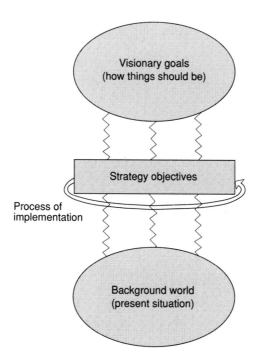

Figure 3-5. Diagram of Objective Concepts

if the attainment probability is zero — then they should not be taken up as strategy objectives.

The second type is the *possibility of implementation*. This tells whether or not means are available for the attainment of strategic goals. In other words, it indicates whether or not you can initiate actions and not whether or not attainment is possible. If the means are not forthcoming, then the possibility of implementation may be said to be zero.

It goes without saying that greater importance must be attached to the question of whether implementation is possible. Goals for which the possibility of attainment is 100 percent have no attraction at all if they cannot be implemented. It is better to do something immediately than to make it into an objective. All that is really needed, after all, are simple instructions for solving it. It is probably true that the more strategy objectives there are, the greater the procrastination of the division head is.

A good strategy objective has high efficiency, even if the probability of its attainment is low (excluding zero). Anything that initiates some sort of action aimed at attainment is of high value as a strategy objective, even if it is difficult. It is also more attention-getting and stirs up the spirit of challenge among members of the division. In the zeal for success, people are likely to opt for comparatively easy goals of limited dimensions. Managers, however, should set their sights on more challenging goals.

Full participation in the division

Strategy objectives should not be made the perquisite of a single person or group. Attainment of strategy objectives requires participation by every member of the division. It is also important for each person to gain a sense of accomplishment. Sometimes division heads make the improvement of their own management abilities into a strategy objective. However, it is difficult to call this a strategy objective. It is probably nothing more than a self-enlightenment goal. Self-enlightenment is an admirable goal, certainly, but one best pursued privately and quietly. It is not appropriate as a division strategy objective.

Making use of resources

Working out strategy objectives demands the investment of all division resources: people, materials, money, and information. Goals that can be achieved through division members' tenacity alone — without materials, money, and systems — cannot become strategy objectives. Neither can goals that emphasize only discussion (for example, holding meetings) and goals that focus only on human relationships. Strategy objectives require larger scale, more dynamic activity.

Clarifying images of achievement

The achievement of strategy objectives must be clearly recognizable to all division members — both those who established the objectives and those who worked toward their attainment. Thus, everyone must share a clear image of the conditions that will exist upon goal attainment. This image will help participants view strategy objectives not as ways of maintaining current conditions but as agents of change. It will also increase their motivation to reach the objectives.

Step 5: Creating an Implementation Process

Obviously, goal construction is more than the mere acceptance of strategy objectives in the division. It requires implementation of activity aimed at the realization of strategy objectives. How do division heads create such conditions? Specifically, what duties and functions must they perform? There are in fact three such functions.

Dream-selling function

The dream-selling function is that of reciting visionary goals. The attainment of strategy objectives cannot be done without the commitment of all division members. And the commitment of division members cannot be gained without a common understanding of the concepts behind those objectives. If these concepts are associated with a current crisis or other negative factor, however, the image of future attainment will be obscured and motivation to achieve goals will be decreased. On the contrary, the concepts behind strategy objectives should be perceived as positive.

Furthermore, division heads must continually relate their own visionary goals in their own words. That does not mean stopping at literature and slogans. Visionary goals should be reflected in the speech and behavior of division heads. Spreading the word on visionary goals elicits understanding and sympathy. A manager should seize every opportunity to do so — the morning gathering, a discussion at a conference, or in a bar — in formal or informal settings.

The way managers express their ideas is also important. To communicate visionary goals, managers should not seek to explain or persuade but rather to narrate. The strength of their convictions will inspire people to act voluntarily.

Some members need no narrative to understand the present. They already know what problems exist and where the causes lie. It is important to receive the recognition of members like that.

Ordering function

The duties of division heads do not end when the visionary goals are achieved. At that point they must give concrete instructions for the attainment of strategy objectives. Rather than remaining silent, they must explicitly tell division workers what to do. They should not turn over to subordinates implementation of something that is only in dream form. Giving orders is not an exercise in splitting hairs. It is specifying the concrete functions in the goal achievement process for each person under one's direct authority. It is clarifying expectations. The ordering function can also be called the idea-selecting function. To make goals attainable, division heads must hand out clear decisions on the various proposals offered by subordinates. Failure to give orders leaves division workers in confusion over what to do, weakens the momentum of achievement activities, and causes a loss of confidence in division heads themselves.

Resource allocation function

Providing and distributing the necessary resources through which strategy objectives are attained is called resource allocation. This may be the most important function of a division head. Achievement of strategy objectives requires more than just dogged determination. Resources must be used effectively. But it is not enough just to use current resources effectively. Managers must also acquire the necessary resources. If certain personnel or skills are needed, then they must introduce programs for such things. They acquire a budget to secure new equipment, or they revamp the organization, until an innovative system is built up. In such fashion, they prepare an environment in which division members can work effectively as they aim to achieve objectives.

In addition, managers must also dare to engage in radical destruction to prepare the environment. If the existing system becomes an obstacle to goal attainment, isn't abolishing such a system the best thing to do? But only the division head can carry out such a destructive act. There is no budget. Managers who fear causing discord among employees will have problems with this task. However, it is impossible to attain innovative goals without causing discord. The fear of doing so is an affirmation of the present, a fear of change.

Division heads who refuse to make necessary changes will be perceived as incompetent and lacking power. By contrast, division heads who fulfill their functions of acquiring the necessary resources for achievement of strategy objectives will inspire subordinates.

By following the above steps, managers can build objectives. Objective building is not simply an enumeration of problems. Neither is it a simple breakdown of organizational goals. Rather, it is a conceptual process.

Through the collision of future energy and historical energy, goals are created. The people who *intentionally* bring about that collision are division heads.

4

Thinking about Strategy from Market Perspectives

Changes in the Market Base

The Advent of Difficult Times for Business

A change in the market base is perceived as a period of upheaval for business. When you think about it, however, change is constantly occurring. Moreover, people are the agents of change. Unlike other animals, we humans progress by making changes.

Given that reality, the problem for business is to attend to the *content* of change rather than the *degree* of change. After all, the degree and speed of change are fairly relative, and because the receptivity to change by the receiving side is also relative, the question of which period has had the most violent change is difficult to answer.

The recent environmental changes for companies began with the personnel labor difficulties and the company defense against the violent postwar labor movement. Next came the storm over rationalization by mechanization, which revolved around machine tools, and the adjustments by the coal mining industry to energy conversion. Finally came computerization and quality control.

The impact of environmental changes on companies has probably been felt in only a few company functions — for example, that of personnel and materials procurement, the hard functions of production and manufacturing, and the soft functions of TQC and computerization of administration systems.

What managers need to concern themselves with is which functions and processes are being affected by current change and which ones will be affected in the future.

Companies are now experiencing perhaps the greatest change of this century: the change in marketing, distribution, and materials flow. Some forty years ago, warnings were already being sounded about the need for a distribution revolution. However, the actual changes made were not of revolutionary proportions, nor were they related to distribution. They occurred in other functions, notably production technology — mass production and quality control. In comparison with the marketing revolution now getting under way, however, these changes may have been no more than a minor wave. Given the ferocity of current changes, difficult times lie ahead for companies.

Decreasing Need for Salespeople

The practice of selling through use of human wave tactics (use of salespeople) has nearly run its course. Until recently, the sales function meant a labor-intensive field that relied solely on a large employee force that went over the market like a roller. Sales management, having remained untouched by the scientific methods based on mechanization, meant simply increasing the number of people in the field. Recent changes in the business environment, however, have made it difficult for sales divisions to carry out their functions solely through the use of salespeople.

For example, in Japan the appreciation of the yen has had a tremendous impact on sales. Yen appreciation used to be a matter for the export department. With the arrival of foreign goods in great quantities, however, yen appreciation has become a serious problem for sales, also. Moreover, it means an automatic increase in Japanese salaries relative to the rest of the world. The average salary level in Japan has already surpassed that of the United States and is now the highest in the world.

Various measures have been adopted in response to yen appreciation. For example, you can capitalize on yen appreciation by converting from domestic to overseas sources for materials procurement. You can also seek low wages and move production sites themselves offshore. Similar measures are considered by every country.

However, procurement of sales personnel from overseas generates problems that are not limited to the legal and administrative arenas. In fact, it would be impossible for foreign salespeople to actively participate in the domestic market, except in the case of special products. Given the tight regional linkages at present, it is clear that the transfer overseas of management organs and facilities, and the remote control of domestic markets will never even become real problems.

What company today has the strength to maintain the largest and most expensive sales force in the world?

The subject of white-collar productivity is hotly debated. The issue is relevant for sales divisions, which are filled with an excessive number of white-collar workers whose activities are highly inefficient.

But that is a subject for another book. The following sections treat the pressing problem of home sales.

The Impact of a Changing Market on Door-to-Door Sales

The practice of door-to-door sales, which began with cosmetics and insurance, is undergoing numerous changes. One factor that contributed to the change was the corrupt commercial practices that led to the Toyota company incident. The subsequent strengthening of regulations has proved effective. Besides that, however, the market itself for door-to-door sales has changed in several ways, each of which will be explored in the following sections.

Repeat customers outnumber first-time buyers

People in the automobile industry now report that some 80 to 90 percent of the customers who buy new cars make trade-in purchases. Only the remaining 10 to 20 percent are said to be first-time buyers. The situation is the same in the housing industry. As a result of skyrocketing land prices, a house in the heart of a metropolitan area is unobtainable by all except the exceptionally wealthy. Even people able to purchase high priced residences face a shortage of housing. The result is that only people who already have houses can afford to buy houses. No way of dealing with this curious phenomenon has yet been found.

Repeat customer demand is also a characteristic of maturing businesses such as those involved with household electrical goods, clothing, and furniture. It is even occurring in consumer goods in the business market.

Customers have changed

Doubts exist about how effective the sales method is for customers who have already bought and used a product. The method used is a variation on the new-customer formula in which the main ingredient is an unannounced home visit. Company training of salespeople emphasizes sales to new customers. As a result, it fails to prepare sales personnel for the actual market, which consists of older, more knowledgeable customers.

Furthermore, as customers have matured, the sales force has become younger. As a result, traditional lines of communication, with sales personnel conveying product information to the customer, have been reversed.

Information media have diversified

The growing circulation of information magazines and the increasing number of specialized magazines concerned with merchandise information such as automobiles, home living, and fashions make it clear that the media through which a customer receives information have become diversified.

The areas of interest taken up by information magazines have also diversified. For example, financial information for the home is now available through *Money* magazine, which sells in supermarkets.

Businesses can now respond to customers in real time through VAN, FAX, and other information resources. The need for sales personnel as information links between the company and the customer is steadily eroding, and it promises to erode further with the development of more sophisticated marketing systems.

Households have changed

With the increase in part-time work, the growing number of employment options for women, and the diversification in labor conditions, it is becoming easier for women to find work. Even when not working, women are more inclined to participate in activities outside the home, such as seminars, golf, or dancing. This trend will likely develop further.

With women no longer at home to receive home visit sales calls, companies are rethinking their sales strategy, groping for a replacement that does not rely on sales representatives.

Even the insurance trade, which relied heavily on personal sales, has started counter sales. Marketing for housing and automobiles is moving toward a more comprehensive strategy featuring a mix of show windows, showrooms, and exhibits.

Surplus of Sales Channels

According to the results of a 1985 survey of commercial statistics, the number of retail stores throughout Japan decreased in comparison with the number surveyed in 1981. The number of wholesalers also decreased overall.

In a debate over the distribution revolution that began around 1955, business analysts predicted a retrenchment among small retailers as a result of the appearance of large-scale stores. They also predicted that the wholesale function would become obsolete. In reality, however, while those merchants went through one period of stagnation, they continued to increase until recently. The 1985 survey results were the first to show a decrease.

If the number continues to decrease, it is likely that the market situation will experience fundamental changes.

One factor behind the decrease is the difficulty in finding workers willing to work in conditions seen in fresh food stores and other specialty stores. Another is the pressure for returns due to the rise in land prices in metropolitan areas. The orientation of customers toward large-scale stores and the intensification of competition are further fueling this trend, a trend that will probably accelerate as a result of new factors.

Increase in distribution inventories

The number of sales locations centering on manufacturers is becoming excessive. Furthermore, the large number of sales locations is also placing a burden on companies.

The biggest problem related to this is the increase in distribution inventories. High-pressure selling is done in the name of goal attainment or to move the steady stream of merchandise being introduced to the market. As a result, the inventory volume within the market has nearly reached its limit. This problem is not confined to sales divisions. The increase in distribution inventories can bring a whole company down, as well.

The reason for this increase is quite simple. Distribution inventories are determined by multiplication of the number of new merchandise items by the number of locations that stock merchandise. If the number of stores handling merchandise increases, and if large numbers of merchandise items are displayed at those stores, then one has the calculating formula by which the distribution inventory totals can increase. To shrink the inventories, you must decrease the number of stores that handle merchandise while reducing the amount of merchandise.

The need for abundant displays of products

But the problem is not solved so easily. The large number of articles listed means an abundance of products on display. That abundance is the attraction of a store.

When consumer demand is constant rather than temporary, the market experiences smooth growth. However, when the market itself has reached maturity, it does not change. In one area of the low-growth retail businesses — the convenience stores and specialized volume sales stores — certain places maintain growth rates two to three times that of others. The biggest factor in their growth is certainly their large amount of merchandise and fine product displays. Seven-Eleven is an example. Customers want to go to a big store with lots of merchandise and lower costs. This makes it appealing. Consequently, people will be attracted to even a convenience store if it offers a multitude of items. Consider again the formula given earlier:

Distribution inventories =
number of locations × number of articles

The number of articles may be thought of as a response to the diversification of needs. An abundant display of products is a necessary condition of selling. A reduction in merchandise items at present would be tantamount to business suicide.

Chain stores for home electric appliance makers and general electric appliance stores now account for less than half of all electric appliances sold. More than half of the electric appliance sales are made by volume sales stores, specialty stores, department stores, and the totally unrelated camera discount stores. The reasons for the poor showing by chain stores are various and complicated, but the primary one seems to be their meager display of goods and inventory. Thus, it is essential to fill stores with attractive displays. If this is impossible to do throughout a chain, then selected stores should be targeted for expansion.

The situation is the same in the market for business products. Indeed, all companies need to control and consolidate their distribution locations.

The "Weakness" of "Strong" Brands

The weakening performance of well-known top brands continues unchanged. In 1988 *Nihon Keizai Shinbun* surveyed market shares for the leading 100 products and services. The top companies took turns with 7 items in 1986 and 5 items in 1987. Furthermore, the top companies experienced a decline in their market shares, with 37 items in 1986 and 29 items in 1987. If the top companies whose market shares remained at the same level are included, it is clear that the top companies are moving around in a state of relative stagnation or decline with more than half of the items.

This phenomenon raises a major issue in the debate on marketing strategy. The traditional strategy is to aim at being first in market share. The logic is that an enterprise with a high percentage share will be able to maintain high profits. A high percentage market share, especially in the top positions, used to be the greatest defense policy in competition. Moreover, acquisition of market share beyond a certain level was regarded as being linked to an automatic increase in market share after that.

All companies now conduct continuous organizational efforts to seek a high market share. Advertising campaigns are based on this aim. But market share is relative. While top companies are struggling to maintain their positions, companies with lower market share positions and recently included ones are competing quite well.

In a mature market, then, the traditional marketing strategy of aiming for a high market share may no longer be effective. Market trends are now completely different from previous ones. It is obvious that companies need to find a substitute for the old, three-pronged marketing strategy of personal sales, expansion of locations, and advertising campaigns.

New Marketing Strategies

Breaking the Shackles of the Past

The first step in responding to market changes never before encountered is to disavow previous activities. Resistance to such a change increases the hold of the past and thus imperils the very existence of the company.

It takes courage to disavow your actions. But in times of a changing market base, a company must do so, and must do so faster than any of its competitors. Well-established companies, which have closer ties to the past, will have more trouble disavowing themselves than lower-ranking and newer enterprises, which remain unfettered by the past and have less to lose by rejecting tradition.

The top makers of lager beer discovered this when draft and canned beer were introduced. They had no sooner branched out to draft beer when dry beer was introduced. The quickness of response to these rapid changes meant success or failure in a competitive market.

Self-criticism gives birth to new things

Market development strategy begins when this raising of consciousness and self-disavowal occurs on a companywide scale.

Imagine the circumstances that would most threaten your company's current goods and services, sales and promotion techniques, and image. Suppose the worst thing is a competitor's product or technology that would make your own marketing system collapse. Next, check to see whether your competitors have indeed initiated such circumstances. If they have, then you must have the courage to embrace an entirely new strategy.

In marketing, an important target for self-disavowal is product planning. Companies that can unleash the development of new products and new technology will force even top brands into difficult struggles. For example, Asahi (beer), Minolta (cameras), and Kao (detergents) are competing well by rejecting technological developments for dry beer, one eye frames, and new, small-size detergents.

Shortening Development Periods

In the final analysis, responding to a changing market is introducing new products that are high in quality. The environmental background to product development has changed, so companies must change their development methods. What successful companies have in common is the considerable quality of their products. State-of-the-art technology — that using biotechnology, lasers, INS, and the like — is less important than solid products based on careful research.

Ultimately, careful management of the development period is imperative. Hastily developed products will lack quality, but a too-lengthy development period will leave a company behind in the ongoing race to innovation.

Management that recognizes its own failures

All companies recognize the importance of product development and technological development, and most invest large sums in resources for that purpose. They continue to do this despite mounting calls for rebuilding a business base and clear evidence that their R&D programs are slow in producing returns. The central problem in development projects is the timing of the delivery period and market introduction.

Managers of the R&D division need specialized skills to deal with its unique problems. They must be sensitive to the temperaments of researchers and technicians, the irregular work methods, and the special concerns of administrators. Furthermore, they must understand that obtaining results does not necessarily mean success. If anything, failures are numerous. The willingness to recognize and act on failure is what determines success.

Clarifying Product Concepts

The task of the product developer is to come up with a product that is absolutely unique. Ideally, it must not only not exist anywhere in the world, but it must also be unimagined by anyone outside the company. Obviously, it is difficult to clearly describe something that no one has ever seen. However, success in development depends on clarification of the product concept, even in hypothetical terms, during the initial stage of its development.

The working methods needed in product development are irregular, and contradictions are common. Early in the development process, the conditions and methods deemed necessary to product development are narrowed down, and a choice is made. Naturally, developers make adjustments to market needs, the sales division, accumulated technology, the market introduction period, competitive products, and other changing conditions. These become prerequisites to that development.

Managers need to be aware of and sensitive to the peculiar features of the research and development division. For example, the work, which is done on a project basis, is ever-changing rather than repetitive. Therefore, management concerns must evolve along the same lines. For example, at the beginning of a project, the overriding concern is basic research, whereas at the end it is market entry, with its attendant issues of sales channels, publicity, and campaigns.

The task of management is to determine the order of the various tasks. In other words, a management strategy that molds itself to the differing features of market, product, technology, and organizational structure is highly effective.

Thus, in managing the R&D division, it is important to assume early on a stance that is suited to the particular product concept.

The Role of Administrators in Implementing Strategy

Changing roles

The role of top administrators has expanded recently in most companies. Whereas traditionally administrators were expected to deal primarily with matters concerning employee motivation and education, today they also need to establish and implement strategies for market expansion and innovative development of businesses. Furthermore, they need to think about how to bring about growth and continuity in the company as a whole.

This expanded role has been necessitated by the dramatic changes occurring in the marketplace. The pace of change is now so furious that those at the forefront no longer have fixed goals in focus. Management through a single dominant personality is no longer effective, as it leaves too many uncertainties and tends to become too removed from the worksite. Administrators are now being called on to think about and act upon the company's management problems.

Old-style managers are no longer needed

The changing economy has also altered the role of managers. Some people believe that the abilities of the managers themselves have declined. Because ability is a relative thing, it is difficult to determine whether this is true. Certainly, however, conditions today are different from what they were in the postwar period, when managers were dealing with a devastated country and a destitute economy. To rebuild and create companies in those conditions required enormous energy, great talent, and unwavering self-confidence. In a period of sustained high growth and stability, the need for such managerial skills is inevitably smaller. Consequently, it is only natural that these skills would decline.

In a business enterprise society composed of motivated employees who are easily supervised, it may be asked what the administrators have been doing until now. Indeed, some managers have hinted that administrators are not necessary. As proof, they point to the success of small group activity. But although autonomy is an important ingredient of success for these small groups, it may be a mistake to underestimate the role of administrators in this movement.

Administrators capable of implementing strategy

Business strategy is considered to be the domain of managers, and so to incorporate administrators into the making and implementation of business strategy, some companies are changing the titles traditionally given to administrators.

New titles include "assistant manager position," "core position," and "management position." Accordingly, administrators are adjusting their skill levels to meet the increased expectations about their roles. Specifically, they are now required to establish and implement business strategy, and to think creatively.

Importance of Strategic Thinking

In both market development and product development, marketing must be strategic in nature. The ability to engage in strategic thinking is a prerequisite for those establishing market development strategies and product strategies. Strategic thinking is conceptual and creative in nature, which makes it different from the more mechanical type of thinking involved in analytical work.

Other points of difference are

- the clarification of goals
- the bias toward key factors
- the utilization of company strengths

A fuller explanation of strategic thinking is given in the sections following.

What Is Strategy?

An explanation of strategic thinking begins with a consideration of the general notion of strategy. Defining strategy is no easy task, however. It is often said that there are as many definitions of strategy as there are scholars. Rather than add to the confusion, a synthesis of ideas is included, listing key points common to the definitions. Strategy is

- responding to changes in the company's external environment
- concentrating on effective areas from a general point of view
- distributing management resources
- instituting structural reform to solve basic problems
- deciding on aims for medium- and long-term periods

Clarifying objectives

When establishing business or marketing strategy, it is essential to first clarify objectives. For example, in the military field, where the concept of strategy was originally formalized, strategy is always based on a clear goal. Usually, that goal is to defeat the enemy. When the enemy is unknown or nonexistent, strategy is neither possible nor necessary.

In business strategy, however, the goals are not so obvious. Often, there is confusion over what goal to find or devise. But unless managers and administrators clarify what is expected of a strategy, what they want to do, and what the limits are in terms of level and scale, strategy will be impossible. Consequently, strategy work begins with the identification of company objectives, business goals, marketing goals, and so on.

Putting conclusions first

Clarifying the goal first may be likened to putting the cart before the horse. Establishment of a goal is the last step in the process of deciding intentions. This process begins with the collection and analysis of information. From the results of this analysis, some predictions are derived. Then one of the predictions is selected as the basis of further activity. The result of that activity is treated as information. This is evaluated so that it may be put to good use at the next decision about intentions. The stages of decision in this thought process result in the establishment of a goal. Thus, the last stage in the process of deciding intentions is the first stage in establishing strategy.

Handling uncertainties

The reason for putting the goal at the beginning of strategic thinking is as follows. The domain of strategy — that is, the company environment of markets, technologies, and competition — is an infinite one. No matter what strategy you use or how much information you process, uncertainties will remain. Strategy is the best weapon against uncertainty. In a perfect domain where all the information was verified, there would be no strategy. Things could be done according to the budget.

Simplifying information

In planning strategy, managers and administrators must simplify the information-gathering process. If they were to pursue limitless information indefinitely, they would not only miss opportunities, but they would never decide anything. Accordingly, they need to narrow down the information to that which is relevant to goals and will facilitate their attainment.

Goals are generally decided on the basis of information gathering, analysis of data, and forecasting. On the other hand, goal setting is the starting point of strategy making. How, then, do managers and administrators determine the goals of company strategy?

The goals of company strategy evolve intuitively, from the values and ideas of the managers. In fact, strategy can be described as a clear statement of the process by which company values and ideas become reality.

Managers with vision

Indeed, the intuitive aims of managers constitute vision in management. This vision is not an analytical thing. It may be called a hypothesis that comes from a manager who has given real structure to managerial values. Establishing this hypothesis and having the courage to clarify it in the form of a vision is called managerial leadership.

The making of strategy demands managerial leadership. If enterprise strategy shows the methods and processes for actualizing vision, then company strategy shows how and by what process the current composition of business activities will change up to a predetermined future period of prosperity. In concrete terms, it is a plan for major changes in the composition of business activities in the next three to five years. Naturally, new and potential activities are included.

However, mere forecasts about natural growth in the current composition of business activities do not by themselves constitute company strategy.

Hierarchy of objectives and strategies

Strategic objectives outside of company strategy can be considered to be occupying the higher levels among strategies. More specifically, a certain business activity will have a strategy, and that strategy will have a goal. The company strategy indicates the conditions for the achievement date of that activity, and normally those conditions become the goal. The relative importance the company gives to that activity becomes a goal. As shown in Figure 4-1, successive tiers, or ranks, are formed. Strategies become goals, strategies aimed at the attainment of those goals are established, and those strategies become goals of strategies at the bottom.

Understanding it in this way, you get an adequate grasp of the relationship between strategies and goals, their overall significance in terms of the company, and the establishment of strategy creation units.

Priority Distribution of Key Factors

In an enterprise that has limited resources, it is impossible to give priority to all activities when developing strategy. A company that distributed the limited resources of management equally among all activities would quickly lose ground among competitors. To stay competitive, companies must concentrate resources, labor, and energy into priority functions.

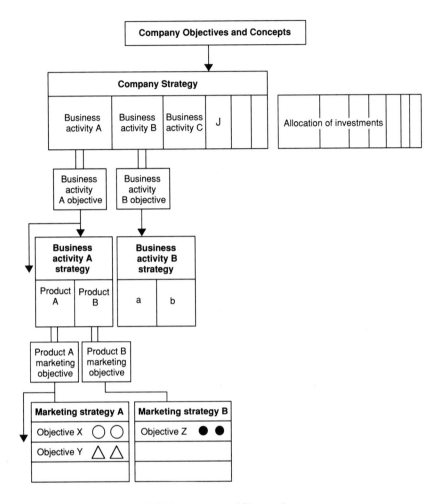

Figure 4-1. Hierarchy of Objectives and Strategies

Strategy aims at imbalance. Strategy is the priority allocation of energy and resources so that objectives may be achieved efficiently and strategy itself may thus be implemented.

Obviously, when a company distributes resources to key factors with strategic effectiveness, it gains an advantage. In competition, the totality of resources does not determine the outcome. Even if the total of all functions and activities a company can mobilize exceeds that of rival enterprises, it will not necessarily win. Rather, the company that is superior to rival companies in just one essential element among the various functions and activities will predominate in the market.

If the total of a company's functions and activities determined strategy, then large companies would certainly dominate the market, and their business activities would be successful. In fact, that is not the case at all.

Strategic success factors

The strategic success factor (KFS) is the key to a successful strategy, and at the same time it is the limiting condition factor beyond strategy in that market. If company managers are unsure about the response to this factor, then success in that market area will be difficult. Thinking about the market response to this KFS is an important activity in strategy making.

Naturally, this KFS varies according to market and product field. Even if KFS predominates strategically in one market, it will not do so in other industries and trades.

There is no strategic success factor common to all markets. Rather, KFS is determined by the specific characteristics of the competitive market. For example, the KFS in automobile marketing is considered to be the number of salespeople and the scale of the dealership. Certainly market share is proportional to the number of salespeople. In addition, while the number of stores does not differ much among companies, there are major differences in scale for any one dealer.

In the soft drink industry, the KFS is the number of sales locations (outlets) and the amount of investment in advertising. In the housing industry, it is the number of display home lots and the number of salespeople. Each industry has its own KFS.

In addition, even within the same industry, the KFS varies. Returning to the example of automobiles, in light vehicles, the KFS is the number of dealerships handling them and the price negotiations. In large-size passenger vehicles, however, name image and quality of a sale are strategic success factors.

Frontal attack and roundabout strategies

In establishing strategy it is natural to begin by seeking out the strategic success factor. For this reason, all companies analyze the functions and activities that are under intense pressure from competition in the market. Thus, KFS can be considered a competitive factor in the market.

There are two ways to approach KFS. One is the frontal attack strategy, in which development occurs through adherence to the existing KFS in the market. The other is the roundabout strategy, which consciously avoids KFS and goes another route. It is never easy to determine which strategy to use, but it is important that you be clear on which strategy has been chosen. In no way should efforts be ambiguous or divided along both paths.

The frontal attack approach to KFS has a high probability of success, but it also carries the risk of placing companies at the mercy of the top companies' strategies. With the roundabout strategy, companies expend considerable effort to achieve success. However, once success has been achieved, it is relatively secure, because the strength derived from a company's own distinguishing characteristics is easily maintained.

Taking Advantage of Company Strengths

The third characteristic of strategic thinking is utilizing strengths. Development of market strategy is done amidst competition. It is not some touchstone by which success is promised upon attainment of a certain fixed level. After all, if competing companies exceed that level, then the company merely meeting it will be behind in the competition.

For that reason, managers should plan a strategy that draws on the strengths of their own companies. That is something that competitors cannot imitate. On the other hand, a strategy that merely corrects company weaknesses will fail. As the saying goes, "All you get from fixing a weakness is the disappearance of the excuse for not fixing it."

In the past, too much of problem solving has been centered on the correction of weaknesses. For example, companies will try to correct in-house problem points or eliminate the causes for an inability to sell. However, problem-solving policies have no place in the sales division or the development division, both of which are strategic domains. Sometimes the problem for which a problem-solving policy is found is not even important to begin with. Furthermore, problem points that remain unresolved create frustration.

Strategy work

Strategy work is analyzing the strengths of your own company and the weaknesses of your competitors. Actually, both analyses are made at the same time. You have to understand the strengths and weaknesses of competing companies in order to understand the strengths and weaknesses of your own company. In the final analysis, these things are relative, measured only by standards set by competing companies. Areas that perform better than those of competitor companies are strengths, while areas that perform worse are weaknesses. In strategy making, then, the analysis of competing companies is essential.

To use the strengths of your own company, you hurl those strengths against the weaknesses of the other companies. This strategy has the dual effect of reinforcing your company's strong points and aggravating the other companies' problem points. This is completely different from treating the problem points in your own company.

Strategic thinking exploits opportunities. When you discover a market opportunity, you bring your company's strength to bear on it. Such opportunities might be missed if you were in a problem-solving mode.

In essence, strategy is an optimistic, forward-looking, opportunistic, creative process. It bears no relationship to problem solving, which is a backward-oriented, pessimistic process.

Hypothetical Approach to Strategy Proposals

To develop strategic marketing, managers have to analyze market information from the three perspectives of strategic thinking just outlined.

They must constantly consider the goal as they collect and analyze information. They must determine the most important competitive factor in the market, and then evaluate their own company's and competing companies' strengths and weaknesses relative to that factor.

From the results of such analyses and evaluations, strategy is established. At this final stage, strategy making requires individualism, originality, creativity, and intuition on the part of managers. To a certain extent, one must be born with these abilities. However, there does exist an approach whose application can facilitate strategy making. This is the hypothetical approach.

The hypothetical approach is a way of thinking that takes as a premise a temporary concept in order to construct a more permanent logic. Analysis and other activities are then centered on such a hypothetical construction.

When creating marketing strategies, convert the goal previously established into a hypothesis; then construct concepts about how to attain that goal.

Specifically, the process consists of the following steps:

1. *Establish a hypothetical goal.* State specifically what the strategy is expected to accomplish.
2. *Analyze company management resources.* Identify those company strengths that will facilitate goal attainment.
3. *Analyze the market for strategy success factors.* Identify the key factors for success in the marketplace. Then measure the gap between the KFS and the strengths of the company.
4. *Create strategic plans.* Construct a hypothetical strategic plan, and then create several alternative plans.
5. *Establish a market objective.* Search for the most appropriate market according to the strategic plan.
6. *Adjust the goal.* Evaluate the possibility of goal attainment by executing the plan in this market objective.
7. *Make the strategy comprehensive.* Restructure the entire strategy according to results of the previous steps.

By this sort of reverse logic, concepts are constructed.

The hypothetical approach to strategy proposals thus facilitates the establishment of strategy while verifying the goal of that strategy. Use of this method also increases motivation for goal attainment and strengthens confidence.

While preparing this manuscript, I came across an article on the train departure bells at the JR Chiba Station. According to the article, nearby residents and passengers complained that the bells, which had sounded for decades to announce train departures, were too noisy. Accordingly, on August 8, the bells were silenced. The station had prepared itself for problems arising as a result of the action, such as passengers missing trains, but not one incident of trouble arose.

For whom had the bell tolled all those decades? In the last analysis, it had tolled only for the railroad workers — not the passengers.

There are undoubtedly similar misconceptions at every company. For example, in the name of the customer-comes-first principle, companies study marketing development. The truth is, however, that this action makes no difference to the customer. Indeed, an all-out effort limited to the logic, customs, and experience of a company can result in eventual losses for customers. I see too many cases in which real losses in merchandise value are caused by the pressure to engage in high-volume sales because of large-scale production. This practice takes from service what it gives to sales.

If marketing managers truly want to satisfy customers, then they should consider what kind of life they would like for themselves as human beings, what things give them satisfaction, and what they can hand down to future generations. They must have the courage to clearly express what they regard as right.

5
Developing Products from the Perspective of Social Needs

The major structural changes facing industry are resulting in the creation of new added value. The significance of this management topic is certainly not limited to the present, but never before has the ability to create business that generates added value been so essential to growth. This chapter explores the development of products that generate that added value by focusing on the training, workshops, and seminars being held at various companies.

The Emergence of New Trends and New Business

New trends and new products can win over a generation. Unless they are perceived to have new value and meaning, however, these trends and products will not generate success. In the development of new business and new products, the road to success begins with an interpretation of the trends (currents) of the times, looking toward the future from the present. This means exploring the meaning of expectations and values contained in new products, structures, and patterns. One of the characteristics of the times, however, is that these trends are difficult to interpret.

Social Trends

The aging of society

It is estimated that after the year 2000, three younger people will be required for the support of every old person. The burden on young people for social welfare and medical services is thus increasing, making it impossible to hope for the kind of growth that we have seen in the last few decades.

Of course, the shift toward an older population has generated new business opportunities as well, with companies attempting to capitalize on the "silver market." Among the products being developed for this market are "all-electronic homes," based on design that is oriented to safety, nutrition, and comfort. These products are based on concepts of "compassion" and "sensitivity to human limitations." However, they do not fully address older people with still-youthful spirits. For those people, products that provide a sense of luxury are being developed. There are also some companies out to get business that is completely different from that of the past.

The increase of leisure time

The Japanese people work too much. They are reported to work 10 percent more than people in the United States and Europe. Gradually, however, they are placing greater value on time spent outside the workplace and discovering the concepts of "my personal comfort" and "my other self."

No matter how you look at it, the life of a person who does nothing but work from early in the morning until late at night is a life without dreams or hopes. While work is referred to as "first time," free time is called "second time." This "second time" offers tremendous possibilities as a market for new business. Expressions such as "fresh time to get back in touch with myself" and "time to accept the challenges of exploring the unknown and unexperienced" are now heard. Businesses that respond to these sentiments will no doubt find success.

The growing prominence of women in society

Armed with impressive academic qualifications, and liberated from the home by new electronic devices, women are increasingly seeking fulfillment in jobs outside the home. Their absence from the home has spawned new business services related to child care and housework.

Because male-oriented attitudes persist even in businesses where women are accepted, however, it is impossible to take sufficient advantage of women's skills and strong points in actual practice. So it has become necessary to rethink job patterns and methods, as well as the equipment, machinery, and tools themselves.

Leaders of one major research center that was designed for male residents were completely at a loss when a married female research center employee requested a company dormitory residence. Such dilemmas were unimaginable until recently. More and more companies now turn to the consulting industry for guidance in such matters.

Changes in consciousness and value judgments

As society matures, the value judgments and goals of the people who live in it become increasingly diverse. An era has dawned in which people are no longer satisfied with the values that makers (manufacturers/advertisers) thrust upon them.

Individual preferences. Many people are demanding products that are tailored to their own tastes. It has become difficult to get customers to pay for standardized, mass-produced products. Accordingly, a custom-order market has emerged. One product of this market is Matsushita Electric's made-to-order bicycle.

Cultural preferences. An example of this is the demand for the reassuring values of tradition in Japan, reflected in commonly heard expressions such as "quiet," "serenity," and "leisure," that signifies a refreshing restoration of humanity in our modern era of violent changes. Also, businesses that capitalize on the interest in ancient culture ("cuisine of the Manyo era," for example) will undoubtedly spring up.

Fad preferences. Consumers who are not satisfied with standardized products are increasingly exercising their own creativity by making things at home. Popular items are homemade light planes and homemade second houses. People are using their brains (to design) and hands (to manufacture) so that they can meet their own specifications.

Stable health preferences. In our modern stressful society, self-management issues such as health control, stress alleviation, and life design have become subjects of greater concern. Because laypeople are ill-equipped to make judgments about health, a new industry in "diagnosis advice" has emerged. The hope is that diagnosis instruments will provide even laypeople with precise advice about the state of their health.

The point in listing these trends is to emphasize the importance of foreseeing future trends in meeting future needs (see Figure 5-1).

Trends in Technology

We have moved from an era of quantitative expansion into an era of qualitative creation. The focus of this new era is on computers and communications equipment, based on electronics. This new technology has been put to the service of precise and creative communications (see Figure 5-1).

Technical change dimensions

In the era that was based on energy, longer-bigger-heavier-thicker systems were generated, reflecting the importance of quantitative expansion (large-scale electric power plants, large-size tankers, and large-scale production facilities). That era was based on the value judgment that "bigger is better." In the current, electronics-based era (semiconductors, sensors, computers), lighter-thinner-shorter-smaller systems with more diversified functions have been produced, the result of the new interest in quality creation. More compact multifunction systems are being created with higher and higher precision. This era is based on a value judgment that "small is beautiful"; therefore, products are becoming ever more compact. It is predicted that there will be another transition, based on biotechnology, as we enter the twenty-first century. Efforts will center on ultraprecise elements that generally have "matter and information and control." This will be a creative period for new technologies and systems. It will produce a new culture and new values.

System structure component dimensions

The year 1985 can be considered to be the beginning of the advanced information society. This is the year when electronics

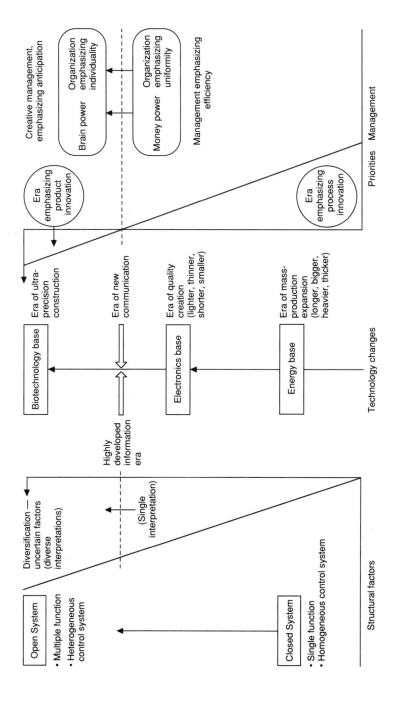

Figure 5-1. Relationship between Current Trends and Business Changes

information networks, combining information with electronics technology, were created. That technology became the mainstream for circulating information in all areas. In many workplaces, paper and pencil were replaced by information machines. Certainly, great changes took place both before and after 1985. The products and systems put together before that date reflected an emphasis on homogeneity, quantity, and power. Yet the functions required in those systems and machines were comparatively simple. They were closed systems whose specifications were relatively easy to decide.

Since 1985, however, the demand for additional functions has increased, and the structural components required for these functions have diversified. So it has become impossible to make such products without the use of heterogeneous technology. Mainstream systems are now those that unify this heterogeneity — for example, mechatronics, optic electronics, and biosensors. Furthermore, they are linked to other systems and they have come to fulfill more comprehensive functions and purposes. Because the subordinate systems (equipment composing the total system, registers for POS system) are regulated by the host systems, the subordinate system specifications cannot be modified without recourse to the host system. In other words, a business must be able to handle host/comprehensive systems if it is to gain a leading position in the industrial world. Otherwise, it will be relegated to subcontracting work. People need to interpret situations and needs flexibly and from a more comprehensive perspective. Management needs multifaceted thinking that can lead to diverse solutions compatible with objectives.

Progress indicator dimensions

During the industrial expansion, businesses made things with an eye to quality, performance, and cost. They also focused on process innovation based on American and European models, asking the question, How can we manufacture things better? Today the emphasis has shifted from "making things better" to "what should be made?" That is because future progress will be impossible if one relies only on conventional products and business. Moreover, the seeds of new products and new business to support the future are not to be found elsewhere. We must find them and with our own hands make them grow. That means that we have to give careful consideration to the following two questions: What should we make? and What kind of values or culture should we offer to society? There are plenty of ideas available for new sources of business; the trick will be to create products and services with high value-added that contribute to basic company business expansion. This is not a simple problem of business or product life cycle. It is rather a problem of coping with a major turning point at the beginning of a new era.

Management dimensions

The effect of the changing business environment on management will be treated in another section, but one point can be made here. To support the kind of product innovation mentioned in previous sections, companies will have to cultivate new management styles. They could combine conventional, efficiency-oriented management — characterized by uniform, organization-centered ideas and capital — with a new-style empowered management. But it would be difficult to combine conventional management with the development of new business or new products. A better idea would be to emphasize individuality in the company and organize intellectual resources. Creative managers must enjoy challenging people and inspiring them to create new plans. These conditions are necessary to an environment in which value-added products can be made.

Expectations for New Products and New Business

The sense of urgency about the need for raw products and new business is particularly acute among manufacturers of conventional products in a mature market. The problems they face are treated in the following sections.

Lack of New Products and New Business

Many companies are initiating projects and forming committees in their search for new sources of business. They often find that traditional ways of doing business have left them unprepared to make the dramatic changes required to stay in business. For example, they may have no sales roots, inadequate technology, or insufficient funds to invest in equipment. Such situations may have been caused by anticipation of a higher success rate than actually achieved, a too-rapid establishment of business, reliance on the skillful imitation of other companies' products, or a lack of experience in generating business ideas.

Whatever the cause, the elimination of such situations inevitably involves taking risks. It also requires recognition of the need to make original products, explore the market independently, consider the needs of the times, conduct an unhurried search for ideas, and devote ample time to their development.

Good Products Do Not Always Sell

Even if companies try to expand business by strengthening existing products, the expected results will not materialize in areas where the market itself is not expanding. That happens when planners and designers neglect to interpret the needs of users and foist a product on the market that users do not want.

Planning should not begin until needs are clarified. After clarifying the targets (users/uses aimed at), companies need to assume the user's perspective to study factors such as lifestyles, purposes of product use, required functions, and performance. The idea is to create products that exceed the customers' expectations in terms of satisfaction. Because it is difficult to step into the users' shoes, many manufacturers assume the users' perspective by considering products made by competitors.

Riskiness of Selling a Single Product at Big Discounts

The lifespan of all products is finite. Thus, a company that sells a single product at a big discount will face serious problems if the product begins to sell poorly. There must be a constant supply of products that can substitute for other products sold at big discounts.

Many companies that are maintaining a strong hold on existing business as well as investing in new business find themselves in a no-growth position. In seeking ways to extricate themselves from stagnancy, they ponder whether to reduce the influence of existing business by boldly forming branch companies or to increase efficiency by, for example, securing stronger support from existing sales divisions.

The Drying Up of Big Business

Companies rarely start doing business on a large scale. It takes time to reach that point. The criterion for judging new business, however, is likely to be the extent to which current business is expanded. Yet the growth projection industries are smaller in scale (see Figure 5-2). Therefore, companies will have to rely on experience and know-how in planning for future business. Careful preparation — the study of other companies, market trends, market position, product specifications, and so on — will be the key to business success.

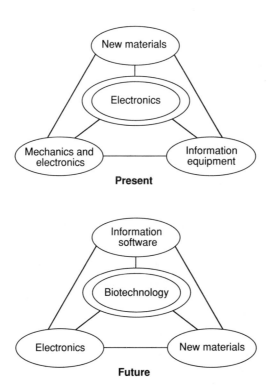

Figure 5-2. Growth Projection Industries — Technology

Riskiness of Making Imitations

The success of other companies is both a strong stimulation and a temptation. It is all too easy for a company to fall into the course of imitating products that have brought another company success. To succeed in this course, a company must have strong sales ability, strong marketing (which can make the desired image penetrate the market), and strong production capacity. Companies that do not have these abilities have to build up their technical capacity, analyze market needs more thoroughly, and develop highly original products.

In the future, however, it may not be possible to quickly manufacture imitations of other companies' products. Because of the new trends in technology, the future belongs to those companies that carefully plan new ventures and then deepen their technological capacity accordingly.

Too Much Cost Competition

The worst-case scenario is one of constant price wars resulting in the elimination of added value. A product will sell when its value is high and its price is reasonable — in other words, when it has good buyer-cost performance. That is,

$$\begin{matrix} \text{product value} \\ \text{(selling conditions)} \end{matrix} > \text{price} < \begin{matrix} \text{cost} \\ \text{(profit conditions)} \end{matrix}$$

When the relationships shown here are in effect, products sell, profits increase, and the business succeeds. This situation can also be indicated by comparing product A's value and price to product B's value and price.

Increasing the value of a product and lowering its price means increasing its overall value. If the value of a product cannot be increased, then the product cannot be sold unless the price or cost comes down. This becomes a worst-case, nonprofit scenario. When such a situation occurs, the use of cost-cutting methods is an important approach. But in order to gain customers, a company needs to increase the value of its product.

Prices are determined by the market. Companies compete with each other by arranging product lines in their respective price zones, but the starting point should be deciding product lines according to the values users of a product want. There should then be communication in a form that the user readily understands. Improvements should be made so that a product's excellence is grasped at a glance. This air of quality should be enhanced upon use of the product.

Anticipating Needs

In product development it is important to turn out products that are clearly distinguishable from the products of other companies. To do this, companies must rethink product concepts, clarify targets, analyze the market and customer situation, and restudy user needs. Product concept comprises fundamental ideas about whether a product satisfies customers and corresponds to their needs. This concept is not just an image that is communicated to customers through catalogues; it is the informing criterion of every stage, from in-house development to sale.

Needs and Seeds

In new product development, both needs and seeds pose a problem. *Needs* are the expectations and requirements of customers. *Seeds* are the technology and materials that manufacturers possess and can provide. Product development begins with a study to determine customer needs. After a product is designed to meet those needs, new technology and materials are developed to make the product. Concepts that begin with market needs are called *needs concepts* (market-oriented), while concepts based on new technology and materials are called *seeds concepts*, or technology concepts (manufacturer-oriented) (see Figure 5-3).

Both are necessary for new product development, but in a mature market where customers are not sure what they want, a new product can arouse demand. So it is necessary to rely on seeds concepts that can awaken subconscious desires among customers. New seeds (technology) thus become the core of product development. But this approach carries major risks because progress is not guaranteed.

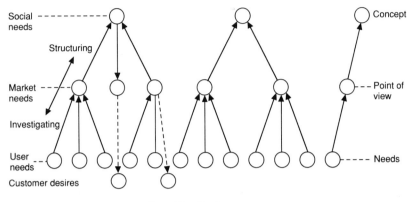

Use of location images

Figure 5-3. Needs Structuring

Although product development based on needs places the company in a more competitive environment, there are fewer risks involved. Manufacturers generally understand seeds quite well; they are in less familiar territory with customer needs. Therefore, a manufacturer-oriented and company-technology-oriented approach to product development is the likely course. However, when both needs and seeds are handled effectively, the resulting products compete well in the market.

Needs Structuring

The current tendency toward individualism has created a market characterized by infinitely varied demands and expectations, with each customer wanting something different. But manufacturers throw their hands up in despair over the prospect of responding to individual needs. Therefore, after structuring the various desires (needs) of customers, they must decide on a development policy to determine what needs should be addressed.

Studies should be conducted in accordance with this method. The first step is to determine what customers are to be targeted by new products. The planners need to imagine themselves as users of the product in question, consider where the product will be used (location), and list expectations (as many as sixty) of the product. Next, they should organize the expectations listed, not according to verbal characteristics or product function, but rather according to how the customer will use the product. The aim is to identify the latent needs of customers by understanding the expectations involved in their demands (see Figure 5-4).

Individual demands are grouped together in a common set of expectations. The manufacturer appraises them in terms of the market, so these come to replace market needs. The superstructure above them shows the market value judgments held in common. It is therefore possible to consider them instead of social needs. By figuring out the needs of customers in this manner, companies can orient new product development to current trends (development of expectations).

Putting Need Before Technology

A product can be defined as something that satisfies human demands or expectations. If that's the case, then the starting point in product development is not the product itself but the demands that give rise to the product. A product that fails to address these demands will likely not sell.

According to Abraham Maslow's theory of human needs, the most basic level consists of bodily needs and requirements for survival. Higher levels of need involve self-realization and individualism. If this theory is applied to society, it may be said that modern advanced industrialized countries are at the demand level corresponding to self-realization. As the demand level rises, there emerges a tendency to attach more value to information than to material things. Thus industries devoted to information and emotion are doing more to satisfy current human demands than are material-oriented industries such as mining. That may be one reason for the huge market in software. Products that eschew the new software-oriented values will lack added value (see Figure 5-5).

Conventional methods based on a technical perspective of product development — with product assembly based on technical logic, followed by manufacturing and marketing — are not attuned to modern sensibilities and markets. Indeed, a technical orientation or a manufacturing orientation is probably behind a product that does not sell.

Arranging points desired in groups

Door opens and closes easily

Door automatically closes when person leaves refrigerator area

Door handle does not get dirty

Door can be opened and shut even when both hands are full

Beer is chilled immediately

Quick freezing does not cause loss of taste

Things can be put in the refrigerator right away, even while still hot

Automatic replenishment of ice

Ice can be made in any shape desired

Transparent ice can be made

Large size accommodates many items

Capacity can be increased for higher price

Internal layout can be changed as desired

Vegetable bin can also be used as a freezer

Temperature within refrigerator can be set as desired

Back is easy to see and reach

Contents can be seen even when door is closed

Method of preventing leftovers

Menu advice for making meals from food in refrigerator

Figure 5-4. A Refrigerator Concept Based on Thorough Grasp of User Needs

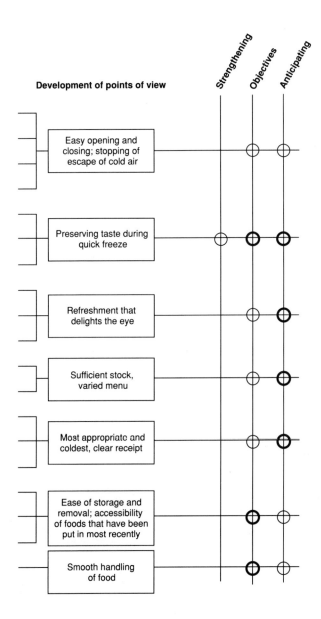

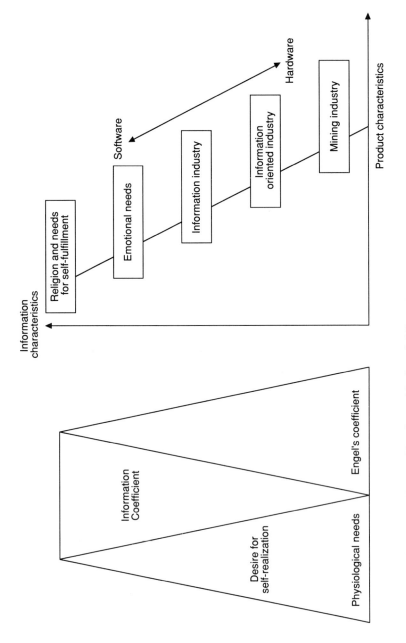

Figure 5-5. Changing Human Needs and Industrial Structure

A product is made according to specifications, but the consumer uses it in the hopes of gaining some benefit from it. People consider products from different perspectives and thus bring different expectations to them. That is why product development must emphasize value to the customer rather than value of the technology involved. The question is not what can be made, but what can be sold.

Systematizing the Development of New Products

There are few companies that work out a system for developing new products and then build on it systematically. The usual process begins with product conceptualization and market research. But the methods for carrying out these steps are generally left up to the experience and intuition at hand. At some companies, new product concepts vary with the individual involved. With a "system" like this in use, there is always a chance that a hit product will emerge, but sustained success is unlikely.

New Product Development Skill

It is said that a product is a mixture of technology and the market. The first stage of its life is development; the second stage begins when it is placed in the market. If the product doesn't sell — that is, if it has no destination — then even a technologically "perfect" item is a failure.

In classifying product development strategy, you make a distinction between products that can be made using existing technology and those requiring new technology. Similarly, you distinguish between products being sold in markets offering current products and those being sold in the hopes of developing new markets (see Figure 5-6).

Improved products result from an improvement strategy aiming to make products better and more competitive in the marketplace, thereby making them more distinguishable from the products of other companies. These improvements involve aspects such as function, performance, design, and cost.

		Technology (seeds)	
		Existing technology	New technology
Market (needs)	Current market		① Improved products
	New market	② Application development products	③ New products

Figure 5-6. Product Development Strategy Classification

Application development products involve a strategy to increase demand through use of current products and existing technology to expand into new markets. This development strategy, often seen in the areas of materials or intermediate materials, is usually an easy course to take because there is such a thorough grasp of the technology involved. But there are many cases where progress does not live up to expectations because of a company's inexperience in the market itself, limited information, and unorganized sales channels.

Sometimes the lack of progress can be attributed to a lack of enthusiasm on the part of the person in charge. But even if vigorous and sincere efforts are made, there will be no success unless market areas are defined and unless full-time efforts are made to cope with the challenges involved.

A problem can also result when leading products are placed in new market areas. It is essential to have a firm grasp on the needs of customers and on the distinction between your own company's products and the products of your competitors. The development of new products means expanding in areas where many technology and market factors lie outside the experience of your company. When this effort is successful, the result is the creation of high value-added.

But no effort to expand will succeed unless bold steps are taken. In other words, it is not enough to devote your spare time to product and market development. Expansion should be authorized and done in a strategic and organized manner, with solid support and strong promotion from each section. After successfully introducing a new product into the market and making sales arrangements, a company needs to develop a stronger sales expansion strategy, making divisions independent as soon as it seems likely that growth can be sustained.

Whether or not a new product will sell well depends primarily on the quality of the product itself, but it also depends on the timing of its introduction to the market, sales know-how and sales channels, and after-sale service. Sometimes companies that are strong in developing technology develop a new product and put it on the market, but it does not sell well because of the companies' lack of sales know-how and selling technology.

In developing a new product, therefore, companies need to organize a solid sales strategy as well as a manufacturing strategy.

As soon as you begin to develop a new product, you need to acquire the know-how, skills, and organization required for implementation.

Application Development Expansion Points

Traditionally, application development strategy has meant expanding demand opportunities, focusing on new markets or on the limits of current markets by taking advantage of acquired technology and know-how as well as products that will expand current markets. Decreasing sales of a product result from demand trends in the market where that product has been introduced. In order to develop a product or technology, therefore, companies must plan expansion by shifting development to those market areas where there is high growth potential. Otherwise, both profits and sales will decline.

Samples of new materials or components with new functions resulting from R&D are shipped to manufacturers, who study their application potential. This method is widely used. Often, however, results do not measure up to expectations.

In conventional new product development, manufacturers take as their starting point new materials or parts, thinking long and hard about what product could be made by using these materials or parts, and what kind of product would result from their application to current products. That strategy succeeded during the time when anything could be sold as long as it was new. But times have changed, and now before making something, companies need to decide what kind of product will sell. Priority has to be given to product planning in terms of the functions and design of the product itself. Then planning must be implemented and the required materials and technology specified (see Figure 5-7).

Samples are therefore delivered for application studies, but application studies alone are not enough to prepare for new markets. Companies also need to study the products of the manufacturers to whom samples are sent and to study the markets involved. What needs will these samples satisfy? What products will they help to make? The ideas and data that offer the best hope of answering these questions should be considered first. Then a strategy for generating application ideas should be devised.

When many kinds of products are involved, materials (M) are processed, parts (P) are made and assembled, and then a function structure (U) is created. After being organized as function structure/subunits (S), the system (T) that aims at unifying them is completed and offered to customers.

The idea generation points are shown in the Figure 5-7 concept chart. For example, when P is developed as a television switch, P's basic function can be expressed as "turning electrical circuits on and off." From the customer's perspective, however,

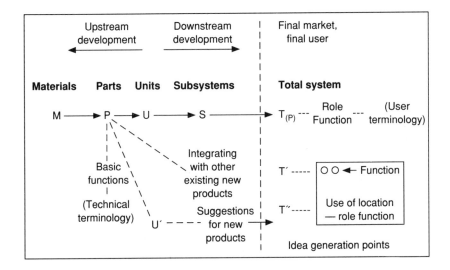

Figure 5-7. Idea Generation Points

P's role function at T becomes "turning the television on and off." That is what the customer is paying for. So there is clearly a difference between the terminology used by the manufacturer and that used by the customer.

Here is a hint regarding the consideration of use applications: When there is a temporary decline in the demand for television sets, there must also be a decline in P and in the production volume to meet the decreased demand. It will therefore be possible to plan selling P by finding a "T that requires P" in other products. The idea for dealing with that situation can be expressed as "turning something on or off," the "something" being an existing product. But let's say the P that is made by competing manufacturers is of good quality. That means it is impossible to enter that market without winning in the competition with that product. The point of entering the market is winning in the value competition. There are many cases where no additional value is produced.

Consideration should therefore be given to adding value to P, and coming up with a new product (T) resulting from either P or U. Thus, companies can increase added value by developing new products that use P and U.

Getting Ideas for New Products

There are many definitions of new products, and if the devices used in sales strategy are included, it becomes even harder to differentiate among them. New products can generally be described as products that use a new technology or that feature new functions. The term can also be applied to products whose technology or functions already exist but are new to the company concerned — in other words, to products entering additional markets. Although such products are not the same as improved new products, they do offer new convenience to customers. Companies that lack experience in both technology and market development and that have an inadequate stock of in-house know-how and information favor this type of new product development.

Thus, much new product development is the result of competition with other companies' products. Nevertheless, to maintain future growth, companies must make sure that their technology functions effectively and that efforts are made to develop new products that are truly innovative.

There are three techniques used to develop ideas for new products: the analogy concept method, the trend concept method, and the newspaper concept method.

Analogy concept method

The analogy concept method is deductive. An ideal image taken from nature is used to generate ideas about the structure, image, and functions of a product.

Trend concept method

There are various factors responsible for the phenomena and needs that arise in society. In the trend concept method, interpretations are made of trends in those factors that bring about past, present, or future changes. Future needs are thus projected, and scenarios are created about the businesses and products that will satisfy those needs.

Newspaper concept method

This is a method for creating an image for a new product. By introducing a new product in newspapers, a company shows the advantages of using it, and this awakens latent needs, further heightening expectations and demands.

All three methods use creative thinking to generate ideas for original products. This creative process must be backed up with the collection and analysis of data, however, so that the issues involved are thoroughly understood (see Figure 5-8).

Developing Creativity Is Essential for Developing New Products

Developing new products requires an accurate interpretation of the trends of the times and a clarification of society's needs and of how to meet those needs. If the company's technical know-how, sales roots, and sales know-how are functioning well, sales will be successful right away. For long-term success, however, the company also needs to offer products and methods that are original and unique. Creativity and the power to generate ideas are essential to this capability.

The Meaning of Creativity

Soh, one of the characters in the Japanese word for creativity, *sohzoh*, means "to wound." This suggests an attitude of healthy skepticism. Creativity, therefore, involves denying the status quo, reconsidering things from a new perspective, and then constructing something. In business, creativity can be defined as an activity that produces original activities leading to profit and efficiency. Unless it involves the creation of new value, it has no meaning.

New value can be classified as scientific value and economic value. Obviously, companies favor economic value over scientific value. But genuine and significant creativity means producing both kinds of value — in other words, thinking inventively about how to

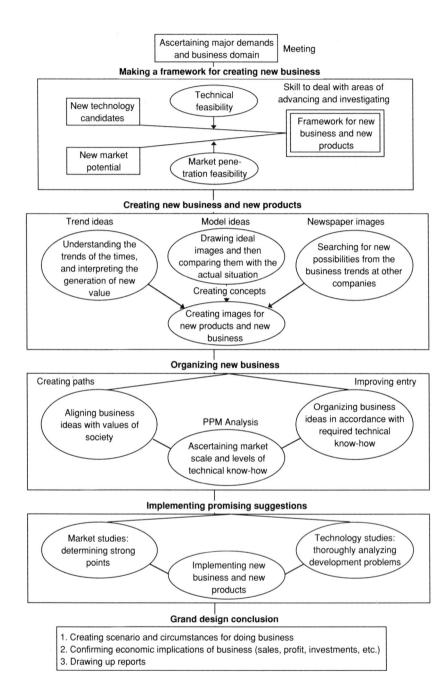

Figure 5-8. Steps for Expanding New Product Development

make those values materialize. In regard to economic values, it means creating methods of implementing profit values. In most cases this means conceptualizing methods of achieving value objectives by combining materials with things that are already known.

In regard to scientific values, the emphasis is on thinking that clarifies the unknown. A systematic explanation results from a study of the cause-effect relationships among fundamental factors responsible for new discoveries or for the construction of things related to them. Evidence is then provided to demonstrate their efficiency, and theories are completed.

In the former case, therefore, the results required for invention are rather clear-cut, with much previously known information and knowledge being used to help form ideas. In the latter case, however, the information is itself rather limited and success or failure is probably determined by factors detected only after the objective is achieved.

Three Aspects of Creativity

Creativity is often considered to be "the power to solve problems" or "the power to produce new ideas." But these definitions indicate an inadequate understanding of creative activity.

Cognitive creativity

Broadly defined, cognitive creativity is the power to interpret socioeconomic or scientific-technological trends. More narrowly defined, it is the power to detect new needs or problems as they occur in the course of your job or daily activities. It involves intuition and foresight, qualities that enable you to perceive something in a way no one else has perceived it. You develop intuition and foresight by continuously asking objective questions, such as: What is happening? and How will things turn out? Discovering needs through the application of cognitive creativity allows you to tap into future demand.

Objectives creativity

Objectives creativity is the power to determine feasible objectives and values. If cognitive creativity leads to a broad interpretation of the needs of society, then objectives creativity defines those needs more narrowly, assigning values to planning topics that correspond to those needs.

Methods creativity

Methods creativity is the power to create the means and methods for achieving objectives. It assumes the existence of both cognitive and objectives creativity, which must take priority in new product development. The first two types of creativity produce varying results, depending on the value judgments and previous experiences of the persons involved. But they rightly place the emphasis on what product *will sell*, rather than what product *can be made*. Another question should be what kind of situation will evolve from now on. These questions increase the difficulties involved because they broaden your perspective. In developing new products or new business, therefore, it is essential to give higher priority to objectives creativity and cognitive creativity than to methods creativity (ideas about how things should be done). Simply collecting information and building up a huge data bank cannot be considered an adequate policy.

Basic Steps for Creativity

Creativity has already been described here rather boldly as an act in which everything is risked for the sake of creating new value. Although even a slight coincidence or minor idea has an impact on society, it is unlikely to increase the business of a company on its own. Creativity lends you the energy to pursue a goal in spite of extreme difficulty. But how is this energy generated?

Figure 5-9 shows a simple diagram of the creative process. Three things are considered at the beginning of creative activities: a is a command or request received from other persons; b is a situation in which the persons involved begin to feel the necessity of what has been commanded or requested; and c is a situation in which the persons involved become immediately interested and willing to accept challenges.

If a (the point where a command is received) is far removed from b (the values, desires, and ideas of the person receiving the

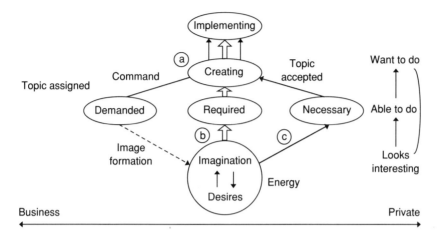

Figure 5-9. Basic Step for Creativity

command), there will be no positive attitude about implementing the command as it was given, and creative energy will not catch fire. However, if the image of achievement and implementation accords with the desires of those involved, both the meaning and the necessity of what is commanded are keenly felt. Thus, the motivation for creativity is adequate. This energy, expressed in the saying "Where there is a will there is a way," activates creativity. In situation *c*, the motivation already exists. Thus, efforts go smoothly and a high level of creativity is achieved.

It is tempting to think of creativity as an accidental process, something that cannot be controlled. The process in *b*, however, is made possible by the conscious acceptance of challenges. First of all, there is an honest rethinking of your own situation. Your own values are formed by sufficient conceptualization of those things you want to accomplish. It then becomes possible to concentrate your energy on implementing them. Creativity is not feasible without an implementation success story written by yourself in terms of your own desires. Even for new product development, if the person involved does not have a clear and strong image of that product's value, it will be difficult to obtain superior development results in situation *a*. Therefore, those involved in new product development should hold discussions and try to refine the product's image until it is in sufficient accordance with their own ideas.

Training Development Personnel

During times of little change, past experience and accumulated knowledge play an important role in product development, because the most effective ideas are those that evolve in temporal sequence. But during times of rapid changes and newly evolving paradigms, information and know-how acquired in accordance with old paradigms lose their relevance. Indeed, what used to be an asset is likely to become a liability if not discarded for new paradigms.

Because beginners (called new recruits by companies) know little about the old paradigms, they can freely approach new paradigms and are more likely than veterans to generate bold new ideas. Their involvement can bring to an organization flexibility, fresh thinking, sensitivity, and the spirit to accept challenges. Those are precisely the qualities needed for new product development.

Use of New Recruits in Product Development

In one experiment, recent graduates of universities were hired by companies not for use in operations divisions but rather for training in business promotion. Four of the new recruits spent a year studying basic information about developing new products and new business, as well as about implementation methods, under the tutelage of their subsection chiefs. They themselves created the search methods for new products and new business as well as the grand designs for marketing (the process is similar to that in Figure 5-8).

The three-month training in basic development consists of lectures combined with hands-on practice, in which senior colleagues also participate. The hands-on training comprises situations of conflict between old and new paradigms; basic training is held twice a month. The young recruits learn to reconcile knowledge gained in school with knowledge gained from experience, and at the same time they discover their own characteristics, value judgments, and ways of looking at the world. The importance of what they have learned from others then begins to come home to them, and they gain self-confidence.

In the second half of the year, beginning in August, they reflect on what they have learned and decide what area of business they would like to pursue, informing the company president of such. After studying trends in technology and new products, market characteristics, and other areas, they begin to generate ideas for new products. The knowledge they acquired in school is worth little without this direct experience to both expand and refine it. Verification of knowledge through experience allows people to define their worldview and to move forward. Moreover, purposeful activity increases extraordinary skills and potential in a short time. When you want to know something, you turn to relevant connections for guidance in proceeding. In the daring spirit of taking risks and welcoming challenges, you construct bold hypotheses and act accordingly.

Of course, uncertainty and lack of confidence are natural in new product and business development, even for highly experienced veterans. And although recent graduates have an academic understanding of technology, they do not understand the needs of society or the process of implementing new product and business development.

However, young people have fresher and more open minds, great flexibility, and a strong capacity to treat new experiences right away as part of themselves. From now on, companies will have to make their development personnel more experienced from start to finish, presenting them with the whole picture at an early stage and developing their capacity to see and judge things more comprehensively. The old methods may make employees more skillful, but they will not foster creativity. *Growth in the twenty-first century will require companies to both accept the challenges involved in changing trends and to themselves generate new trends.*

6

Activities that Bring Out
Maximum Energy

Developing Business Innovation while
Using Maximum Energy

The Power of Small Group Management

Social trends are gradually moving out of the confused, chaotic situation of the recent past. Management activities can take advantage of this emerging stability to concentrate the energy of the company for optimum growth. This opportunity to revitalize comes with some problems related to restructuring an organization to release its creative potential. Managers must avoid confusing these new management problems and the evaluation of present circumstances as the result of accumulated efforts of the past. This could result in a total rejection of the former way of doing things and cause further anxiety and confusion within the company and in relations with affiliated companies. Nevertheless, if people insist on doing things the old way in the midst of current change, it will be impossible for the company to survive. Then how should activities that concentrate on maximum energy like small group management be promoted?

Managers need to understand the principles of small group activities and the evolution of small groups within their own companies.

Small group innovations form the core of management development. If the activities are handled properly, they can buck current trends and chart new territory. There are a number of reasons for the growing importance of small group management.

Results factors

Human resources are the basis of management. Efforts to improve management naturally affect the ability of people to do their jobs. People dislike the strictures of excessive control. Therefore, companies have turned to small group activities as a way of transferring authority or decentralizing divisions. This may be referred to as the vertical formation of small groups. The division of large groups into smaller groups is the horizontal type of formation. Each type should be used in conjunction with the other (see Figure 6-1).

Information factors

The basic conditions for the flow of information are the shared characteristics or balance in qualitative and quantitative tendencies between the communicating party and the receiving party. Another condition is the existence of common evaluations and value judgments about work. The larger the group, the more difficult it becomes to achieve this shared, or consensual, quality. The smaller the group, or the more effective the system constructed, the faster and more accurate the flow of information will be.

Information means all the data required to make goal achievement possible. Obviously, a primary management goal today is to improve efficiency in terms of information quality and information flow. Thus it is essential to establish information flows and systems that link small groups together.

Knowledge factors

Recently, production and delivery times have been getting shorter. Thus, new technology and techniques have had to be developed so that original products could be created quickly and constantly.

The new knowledge resulting from this situation has been loudly proclaimed as a major factor in leadership of the 1990s. The proliferation of technology and products has created the need for management by small groups, which bring together individuals of complementary characteristics for the purpose of generating maximum energy and combining many skills effectively.

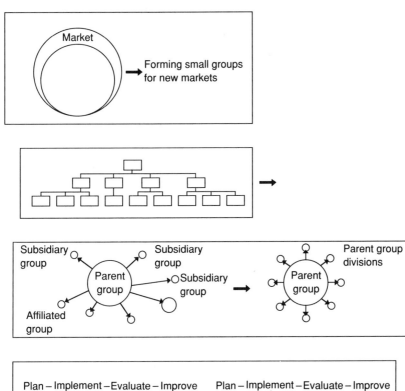

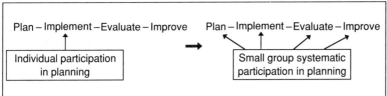

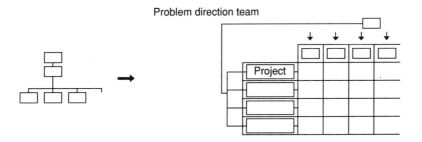

Figure 6-1. Small Group Formation Tendencies

Along with small group management have come small group operating procedures and techniques for combining them, or management technology. This is needed not only in job definition, R&D, and planning but also in production and many other areas that affect management.

The recent tendency to make a rough division of management functions and assign information-gathering functions to a specific division has proved inadequate for responding to changes. This has resulted in the gradual formation of information-gathering techniques that focus on individual persons in accordance with small group management.

What Is Maximum Energy?

Many companies have made use of small group energy and are continuing to expand the various activities and exercises. They use a variety of names to describe them, such as ZD exercises, QC circle activities, and project teams. Although the small groups have different objectives, contents, and methods, according to their respective corporate cultures, they have the common aims of maximizing energy, increasing efficiency, and improving human relations. They also share occasional failures in activities directed toward those ends.

The following sections define more closely the terms *small group* and *maximum energy*.

Changes in Small Group Research

More and more people have come to consider small groups and teamwork as methods of protecting organizations against inflexibility. The United States and Europe, whose urban and machine cultures developed early, are particularly interested in small group research. Figure 6-2 lists small group research trends from 1898 to 1955. According to this table, the prewar small peaks occurred during 1933 and the period from 1937 to 1939. But the lion's share of small group research occurred after 1946, during the postwar period. (Since *Small Groups* was published in 1955, the figures for 1954 and 1955 are perhaps not entirely accurate.)

Year	Number of Books	Number of Articles	Year	Number of Books	Number of Articles
1898		1	1936	1	
1902		1	1937	3	10
1904		1	1938	3	9
1905		2	1939	4	14
1909	1		1940		10
1911	1		1941		11
1912	1		1942		15
1920		2	1943	2	6
1924	2	3	1944		10
1925		1	1945	3	5
1926		1	1946		6
1927	1	4	1947	4	12
1928	2	3	1948	5	25
1929	1	6	1949	2	23
1930	1	6	1950	10	43
1931	2	2	1951	10	73
1932	1	8	1952	10	61
1933	3	12	1953	6	72
1934		3	1954	2	35
1935		5	1955		3

Figure 6-2. Small Group Research Trends

There were a number of factors fueling interest in small group research after the war.

1. Detailed studies of Shaw's thrasher flow and White's friendship groups and gangs
2. Increased experimental small group studies and a group dynamics periodical called *Human Relations*
3. A journal called *Sociometry* heightening interest in group therapy
4. Group discussion and group counseling in education, and group work and community organization as tools of social work and welfare
5. A revolution in personnel management methods prompted by intensified international competition and an expansion

of organization development (OD), ZD exercises, QC circle activities, and other small group methods
6. Leadership training to improve efficiency of all group
activities
7. Group techniques for dealing with large numbers of people simultaneously, adapted by companies from the military and from medical therapy

The Combined Energy of Small Groups

A small group is often defined as a unit in which a small number of members are joined together. A group is a "gathering of
individuals," but the sense reserved for "small groups" differs from
the sense given to "crowd." A crowd is a gathering of people that
is accidental and temporary, without intimate relationships among
its members. A group, on the other hand, is a gathering of people
who have specific goals and who are organized for a specific period
of time. Moreover, the members of a group often interact closely
with each other and are aware of each other as colleagues. They
have a group identity.

In sociology, groups are generally classified into various types
(see Figure 6-3).

Among these types, an organized group can be called a group
in the strict sense of the term. Tonnies's division between
Gemeinschaft (community-oriented society) and Gesellschaft
(profit-oriented society) is well known, but other, lesser-known
classifications are also included.

Conditions for forming small groups

Small groups are characterized by direct mutual interrelationships among their members. In this sense, they are close to primary
groups (see Figure 6-4). However, when they are organized by
management, they are often closer to secondary groups. Small
groups are essentially organized units involving interactions among
the people who participate in them. In other words, they involve
cross-sectional concepts of a process of social action actually carried out by the people themselves.

Assuming that there are differences of degree among small
groups and that their members interact with each other, it is suf-

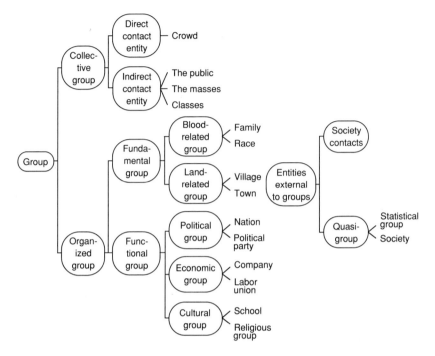

Figure 6-3. Group Types

[• Primary Group
L • Secondary Group
[• Psychogroup
L • Sociogroup
[• Informal Group
L • Formal Group
[• In Group
L • Out Group
[• Reference Group
L • Membership Group

Figure 6-4. Important Factors in Small Group Structure

ficient if there is some kind of dynamic process maintaining cooperative social actions. Depending on how they are perceived, groups are classified as primary or secondary, formal or informal, and so on, in accordance with levels of interaction among their members and levels of social action. But all are groups comprising the smallest units of multi-person social behavior.

Although they contain few members, small groups are the human behavior units with the most intimate interaction among members. The following conditions are generally required for small groups:

- direct relationships among members
- interaction among members
- shared impressions and perceptions among members

A small group is defined not by the number of members but by the interaction between members. Thus, even a group of 30 to 40 members can be called a small group if members are in close and intimate contact with each other on a daily basis. When groups become too large to support such intimacy, they often break up into smaller factions.

A more detailed analysis of such small groups reveals the following conditions:

1. common goals and objectives
2. face-to-face interaction, that is, stable and continuous interactions among group members
3. results showing that group members are organized with clearly defined roles
4. group members participating in similar group activities
5. existence of standard behavioral patterns or norms
6. sense of group identity among members

Small groups have a clear cohesiveness as well as a certain congealed quality. That is, the unity of members is strengthened by group consciousness of goals and standards. While this contributes to maintaining group homogeneity, it also encourages exclusive and conservative tendencies to develop.

Limitations of some small groups

The so-called bureaucratization phenomenon results when management becomes top-heavy and small group functions become overly rigid. This generally results in various problems such as inefficiency, too many employees, accidents, and low morale. Two types of small groups are usually formed to combat this phenomenon, each with special features and limitations.

Committees. To prevent divisional factionalism, companies often form standing committees that span all divisions and handle functions such as mutual opinion coordination, advice, and surveys.

Although I do not have enough information to judge their management methods, I can address one of their limitations. Often, the scale of these committees is too small to permit the participation of all employees in planning, so the committee becomes in effect an elite group. This is a limitation in situations where fuller participation is desirable.

Project teams and task forces. Divisions are often organized in such a way that the restrictions on personnel, authorization, and communication obstruct idea development and product development. Accordingly, project teams are often formed to carry out specific tasks and plans by bringing together people with special skills from many divisions. In other words, a project team is a small group formed to promote a specific project. It should be distinguished from a task force, which is a large group formed in a similar manner to promote a specific project. In Japan, many of these task forces are formal organizations for promoting large-scale plans that cut across divisional boundaries.

Although a project team is usually an informal organization for carrying out plans within a division, it often bears more resemblance to a formal organization. One of its limitations is that it easily develops into a compulsory framework with the norms coming from above, rather than one with individual spontaneous participation in planning.

Advantages and disadvantages of small group (maximum energy) activities

When deciding whether or not to use small groups in various situations, managers should consider their advantages and disadvantages. The advantages are as follows:

1. The members of small groups can contribute various material and ideas, so much information can be combined and many ideas generated.

2. Members have equal opportunity to come up with good ideas, a system that encourages weaker persons and corrects individual prejudices and excesses.
3. According to the old saying, "Two heads are better than one," when combined, ordinary ideas may become extraordinary ideas.
4. Because idea generation is a joint effort, self-esteem is preserved and the results of ideas can be regarded as spiritual resources held in common.
5. When the goal is adapting to what is practical, the results of group ideas can be used to determine the roles and responsibilities of each person to most efficiently accomplish what needs to be done.

The disadvantages of group activities (areas where individuals function better than groups) are as follows:

1. The decision-making process is too drawn out when decisions that can be made quickly by individuals are made at the group level.
2. Group efficiency decreases if any group members are uncommitted and unwilling to take responsibility.
3. Unity and control are difficult to achieve if any group members insist on getting their own way.
4. Opportunities are missed when wasteful activities are conducted and decision making takes too long.
5. Misguided actions sometimes result from the application of a compromise to a situation that calls for a black-and-white decision.

In short, it is necessary to have an adequate understanding of both the positive and negative aspects of small groups and to study group formation and management accordingly. A comparison of various small group activities in Japan can be found in Figure 6-5.

Case Study in Use of Small Groups for Maximum Energy

Concentrated Strength Exercises

During the last several years, much attention has been focused on company management as a problem of organizational strengthening. Small group activities are viewed as important elements in such strengthening.

Consider the small group activities, or "concentrated strength exercises," of company T.

One of the management objectives at company T was cost reduction. This was not just a theme for discussion; it was a key management problem. After instructions were handed down, concentrated strength exercises were begun at each factory. All employees at the worksite participated in problem-solving activities designed to reduce costs. The idea was to get worksite employees to distance themselves from their jobs and form small groups. Discussions were an important part of the exercises, as they encouraged participation and spontaneity by all members.

Today, 250 small groups are engaged in a range of activities at company T. They are autonomous worksite organizations with expanded job classifications. Even if the worksite director becomes a group leader, there is no imposition of authority on the group. The leader's role is limited to creating an environment that fosters leadership qualities, thus making it easy for all members to participate in activities.

The *steering committee* is a standing committee responsible for planning, promoting, and evaluating concentrated strength exercises. Group leaders are members of the steering committee. The steering secretariat is based in the general affairs section, and the person with overall responsibility for activities is the section chief of the general affairs section.

One small group at company T worth noting is the *inquiry group*. This group solves problems that occur as activities expand.

	QC Circle Activities	ZD Exercises
Specific Features	Emphasize people; are supported by in-house education; are based on specific methods; satisfy the requirements of Q (quality), C (costs), D (volume), S (safety), M (manpower)	Emphasize psychological aspects of group; motivate people to do jobs correctly; satisfy the requirements of QCDSM.
Evaluation	• Each company establishes and implements its own methods without proposing a unified evaluation system. • Many companies combine a group suggestion system with the existing suggestion system. • Evaluation is often linked to an existing award system • There are many opportunities for trainees to give talks at national conventions, in-house experience presentation meetings, and other gatherings.	• Personnel records are separated from zero defects performance evaluations. • A suggestion system is established for eliminating the causes of mistakes, while maintaining the existing system through which improvement suggestions are implemented. • A separate zero defects award system for bonus awards is established.
Efficiency	1. Independent activities 2. Specific activities	• self-study (for self-fulfillment) 　— activates latent talent • relief of monotony on the job (self-related desires) 　— increases self-confidence, capacity for independence, knowledge, technical skills 　— increases sense that one is respected by colleagues • contribution to the company (society-related desires) 　— increases sense of belonging, sense of solidarity • thorough planning of policies and goals • improvement of quality maintenance • cost reduction • increase of production volume • improvement of quality consciousness (general morale) • establishment of solid management, restraints

Figure 6-5. A Comparison of Various Small Group Activities in Japan

History	In 1962, as part of companywide quality improvement activities, many companies in Japan formed QC circles and followed the guidelines set down in the journal *The Worksite and QC*	In 1962, American company Martin Marietta introduced a ZD program for its rocket program, as part of quality control activities aiming at zero defects. This was followed by the adoption of ZD in GE (1963), the U.S. Defense department (1964), and Japan's NEC (1965). Thereafter it spread throughout Japan.
Basic concepts, characteristics, goals	• A small group independently carrying out quality control activities at the worksite • Thorough planning of top-level policy as part of companywide quality control • Solid management at the worksite; thorough quality assurance • Increasing management skills of front-line supervisors • Full participation and cooperation at the worksite; companywide implementation of QC • Enhancement of quality, costs, problem consciousness, and desire for improvement	Focus on customer through efforts to obtain zero defects, reduced costs, and reliable delivery. • Management of goals through proper motivation of operators • Development of responsibility as well as creativity in problem solving • Encouragement of personal growth • Promotion of expansion and profit through improved skills • Motivation of workers thorugh ongoing exercises
Factors	• Cooperation and participation of all workers • Enthusiasm, desire, quality consciousness • Strengthening and stabilization of management • Solid improvements in perseverance • Creative ideas • Planning • Permanent problem consciousness • Independent management • Independent inspection • Education, training, SD • Workers educating each other	• Importance of work becomes clear • Group goals are set and efforts made to eliminate the causes of mistakes • Awards given for results • A gradually emerging recent tendency: QC + CD = QZ
Organization	Usually informal with group leaders and operators working at the worksite QC circle headquarters is located within the Nikka Giren, with 7 branches throughout Japan	Activities are carried out independently; promotion organizations are closely linked to the administration

	Suggestion system activities	Autonomous management activities
Specific features	Suggestion activities carried out for the purpose of • shortening time and improving operation methods and processes • improving equipment for functions such as machinery installations • generating ideas for economizing on labor, materials, and other expenses • generating ideas about new products • generating ideas about improving administration efficiency • improving quality • generating ideas about improving environmental factors such as safety and hygiene	Management through promotion of independence, full participation in planning, self-improvement, and mutual education; establishment of relevant topics; analysis of current conditions; setting of goal values; establishment of activities plans; identification and analysis of problem; implementation of countermeasures; efficiency confirmation; restraints and standardization; complete reports and announcements; autonomous management activities bonuses
Evaluation	Using uniform evaluation standards, the evaluation committee adopts or rejects proposals and assigns award levels.	As a rule, the committee evaluates levels of individuals and small groups, treating subjects as suggestions. (Autonomous management activities suggestions — small groups) • Evaluation emphasis: problem consciousness 25% / level of effort 50% / efficiency 25% (Idea suggestions -- individuals) • Evaluation emphasis: creativity 25% / effort 35% / efficiency 40% (Invention improvement suggestions) • Evaluation emphasis: originality 40% / effort 30% / efficiency 30%
Efficiency	• Increase job satisfaction • Increase worker self-confidence and enthusiasm for worksite activities • Generate suggestions that contribute economically efficient management • Foster sense of achievement	Develop individual creativity and increase value of work, thereby increasing sense of individual value • Contribute to company efficiency • Support administration functions • Create a sense of solidarity in the worksite

Figure 6-5. (cont.)

History	During the reign of the 8th Tokugawa shogun, Yoshimune, the "Meyasubako" was created to reflect the will of the people in politics; around 1951 the chairman of Toyota Motor Corporation visited Ford Motor Company and observed its "suggestion system," which was the impetus for the system's introduction at Toyota and in Japan. Other Japanese companies soon followed suit. • 1951, Toyota Motor Corporation • 1952, Canon • 1954, Sanyo Electric, Tokyo Gas, Nihon Pistons, Kubota Steel	Independent small groups — such as QC circles, ZD groups, and no-error activities — were included within the framework of already existing activities, their aim being to establish independence. The entire steel industry engaged in activities called independent management activities. • An independent management activities committee was established within the Japan Steel Federation to promote activities • In 1968 the Japan Steel Federation established the term *JK activities*.
Basic concepts, character- istics, goals	• Intended to provide educational and spiritual efficiency, generating a desire for constructive improvements • Encourage positive thinking and creativity • Intended to increase efficiency through suggestions • Intended to improve morale and human relations at the worksite through improvement suggestions	• People at the same worksite or performing in the same kind of work form small groups, select their own leaders, set goals independently, and then conduct activities designed to achieve those goals. • Improve leadership capacities of supervisors • Improve morale of all employees (quality problems, improvement consciousness improvement) • Unify daily work functions of managers and operators throughout the company
Factors	• Promote spontaneity, creativity, and problem consciousness • Implement many systems attuned to other small group activities	• Promote leadership • Promote self-improvement • Promote consciousness of quality, problems, improvement; thorough implementation of top manage-ment policies by subordinates • Improve productivity • Improve CD • Solidify management • Enhance quality assur-ance, preventing mistakes • Improve yield • Improve operation rate • Eliminate defective goods • Maintain worksite environment
Organiza-tion	Cooperation and promotion of daily work among all employees; participation at the individual level; increase the number of chances for suggestion competition within the company	Leaders range from supervisors to candidates forming small groups with subordinates; with company, without pressure from superiors

	Exercises for zero accidents
History	In 1973 the slogan "all employee participation for zero accidents" was proposed as part of an effort to improve safety and hygiene in the workplace. A zero-accident promotion headquarters was established within the Central Labor Accident Prevention Association as the main organ for achieving this.
Basic concepts, character-istics, goals	(Concepts) Management has a basic responsibility for the safety and well-being of human beings: (1) zero principle, (2) priority principle, and (3) exchanging ideas of participation by all employees.
Factors	(Principles) Progress through participation: based on: (1) project team principles, (2) agreement principles, and (3) family meeting principles
Organization	Small group complex and mobile system is organized according to three main zero-accident factors: 1. Top management situation 2. Thoroughly organized lines 3. Worksite independent activities

Specific features	(Contents of activities)
	1. Setting goals (group decision)
	2. Detecting and eliminating potential accidents
	3. Analyzing accident examples
	4. Drawing up and improving operation standards
	5. Engaging in independent activities based on creative ideas
	  • creating an arena for accident hygiene
	  • holding vertical and horizontal discussions
	  • aiming for innovations in the management climate
	
	(The logic of problem solution)
	1. Posing problems
	2. Grasping the actual situation
	3. Searching out (basic) causes
	4. Creating solution scenarios
	5. Analyzing case studies
	6. Making actual evaluations of conclusions

Evaluation	Based on qualitative and quantitative aspects of efficiency results of exercises and changes in attitudes
Efficiency	Increases awareness of labor safety; lowers accident rate by a significant degree; increases worksite efficiency

Figure 6-5. (cont.)

Its members are high-level specialists, and section chiefs and sub-section chiefs serve as its leaders. The group functions as a task force trying to implement various improvement suggestions resulting from concentrated strength exercises (it is difficult for groups to solve problems, so one of its major objectives is solving problems at the company level).

Specific Efforts to Cut Costs

To implement concentrated strength activities, factories have a "cost-cutting manual" drawn up and distributed beforehand to each worksite. This functions as a guide explaining what points should be studied and what challenges accepted. The meaning of cost cutting can be interpreted broadly. For example, exchanging the greeting "good morning" is a type of cost cutting. If the morale of employees is raised by a greeting, their productivity increases, and this results in a reduction of costs.

Each group uses discussions to decide on group objectives and members' roles, but in the beginning does not make difficult decisions. It is deemed better to deal with problems close at hand and to set simple objectives that can be achieved with a little effort. The basis of concentrated strength exercises is that their specific and practical common goals allow the members involved to maintain peace of mind and composure in dealing with each other.

Results of Concentrated Strength Exercises

It hasn't been long since exercises began at company T, so it is too early to discuss concrete results. But I asked a few persons about their ideas and expectations regarding these exercises.

The factory director, representing the factory, responded in an address to workers: "Our company's long-range management planning is concerned with increasing efficiency, profits, and wages while maintaining steady employment. In order to achieve these objectives, we must link the unlimited growth of our company to the happiness of its employees. Concentrated strength exercises provide all of you with meaningful work and a worthwhile life. That is why the strengths of our employees must be concentrated in a unified way."

Management orders to cut costs and increase efficiency go only so far without worker commitment to those goals. Moreover, if all workers concentrate their energy on single goals (use maximum energy), they will begin to achieve them.

The production division at company T soon began establishing one record after another. Many unique improvement suggestions began to appear, and improvement movements emerged everywhere.

One caution should be mentioned here. Although companies should attach fundamental importance to problem-solving techniques, they should take care not to overemphasize those techniques. Otherwise, competition over techniques will supersede the main goal, which is to make all employees capable of applying limited and efficient techniques in any situation. The emphasis should be on the know-how and psychological aspects of participation in activities.

Strength concentration exercises, firmly based on such factors, are group activities that tap into long-term latent energy. The idea is to understand actual conditions through careful communication. Accordingly, exercises facilitate the sharing of information related to questions, such as: What should be done at the activities site? How should it be done? and Is progress being made?

In regard to the future progress of strength concentration exercises at company T, the steering secretariat staff made the following statement: "The progress of group activities does not depend solely on psychological factors. There should also be a thorough grasp of the importance of cost factors and currency exchange rates. Problems addressed by small groups should be those held in common by members. At discussion meetings, members work out a policy for solving the problems." There should also be a realization that the steering secretariat must ensure thorough follow-ups.

Because the skills of group leaders are now especially important, company T is investigating ways to implement quality and enrichment training for group leaders. The following statement was made on behalf of the group leaders:

> The purpose of strength concentration exercises is
> to funnel the individual strengths of workers into the

common goal of solving worksite problems. Workers are released from formal job structures so that they may form small groups. Group members hold discussions to examine problems that they themselves have detected. The smallest accumulations of such activities become common objectives for the entire company and contribute to the overall effort to reduce costs.

The exercises at company T have raised morale in all levels, from top management to front-line workers. Efforts to broaden the scope of activities to affiliates are now under way. In the words of one group leader:

> There is nothing to be gained from the attitude that the worksite belongs to the company while work is done at the behest of superiors. This dry-as-dust approach removes initiative from workers and turns the worksite into a place of pain. By contrast, strength concentration exercises are based on the freedom and independence of workers. The choice of activity over passivity, self-management over authoritarian management, affects the essence of the work itself. The work becomes enjoyable. A sense of enthusiasm, unity, and cooperation develops.

Those words express some of the basic conditions for small group activities that utilize maximum energy.

Future Prospects for Small Group Activities

Recent Developments

Since 1975, an increasing number of small groups have expanded their activities by setting concrete, quantifiable goals while trying to clarify contributions to productivity improvements. Also, activities promotion organizations have become prominent at worksites. Both of these developments indicate a growing tendency to emphasize actual results. Among the various factors behind this trend are the problem-solving orientation, complementary functions, and group management style of small groups today.

Clarification of small group objectives and emphasis on problem solving

As mentioned, there has been a growing tendency for small groups to set concrete, quantifiable goals related to cost reduction and quality improvement. So-called problem-solving activities have become mainstream in companies.

Small group members select objectives that support company objectives of improving productivity and efficiency. Even though small group activities are carried out independently and spontaneously by worksite regular employees, they are still carried out within a company framework. Figure 6-6 shows the links between small group activities and more formal systems in the company.

Because overall authority rests with the company itself, it is only natural that input into company activities would be strongly oriented toward the company goals of improving productivity and efficiency. This is true of all activities, no matter how far removed they are from the scope of regular work.

Actually, small group activities have increasingly entered the mainstream of company work. People who contribute to the success of small group activities feel proud of their efforts to improve productivity, and at the same time they receive formal recognition from the company. The contribution of small group activities to company well-being is thus highly significant (see Figure 6-7).

Complementary functions and group management

The recent dramatic changes in the company management environment, which include the changing value judgments of workers and the increasing influence of performance management, have been linked by some to a weakening in the group orientation so characteristic of Japanese management. This would mean a decline in unified attitudes about the company and in group solidarity at the worksite. If this is true, then small group activities have an additional advantage of countering these trends with an efficiency that complements and strengthens the basis of cooperative management.

When small group activities support company goals, people at the worksite gain a sense of concern about performance at both

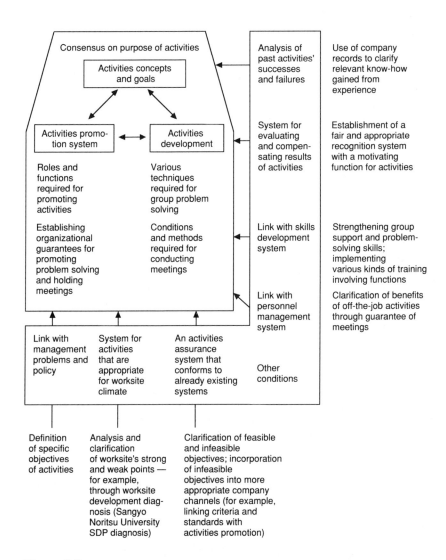

Figure 6-6.

the worksite level and the company level. Such concern strengthens solidarity at the worksite and in the company while increasing job motivation and thereby improving efficiency. It is no wonder that small group activities are gaining prominence in companies today.

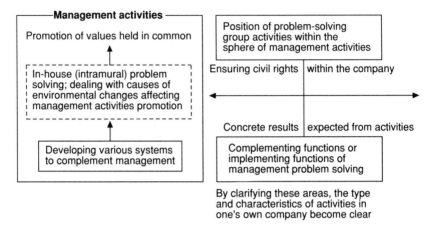

Figure 6-7. Small Group Activities as Part of Company Framework

Problems and Future Growth

As mentioned, the problem-solving type of small group activity that reflects the management environment has gained favor. There are problems associated with this type of activity, however, which could affect its future.

Uncertainty about job security

Despite the decline in a sense of identification with the company among Japanese workers, Japan still maintains a high level in this area when compared with other countries.

The life employment system is a major factor in the strong ties between the worker and the company. Indeed, it has sustained group-oriented management throughout the recent turmoil in company management. Although small group activities are intended to complement cooperative management, if the life employment system falters severely or collapses, group-oriented management will also stumble. The activities themselves will then be called into question.

In the wake of the 1973 oil crisis, many companies embarked on a process of organizational reform. They redeployed personnel as part of their program to implement management rationalization and reduction. From now on, scrap-and-build policies coupled with redeployment will be a matter of course. So will an emphasis on skills, introduction of retirement options, and more conspicuous turnover of employees.

For small group activities to be productive, members must be unified to the extent that they can work without worry. Lack of confidence in job security and an ever-changing roster of members will distract the group from the task at hand.

The role played by middle-aged and older workers in promoting activities is quite significant. Whether or not those workers participate in activities as group members, they still expect to be at the spiritual core of those activities, providing everything from promotional help to technical expertise. When their expectations are fulfilled, their self-esteem increases. But if they are worried about job security, their self-esteem will suffer and thus so will the small group activities. The life employment system is particularly important to the older workers.

The necessity of developing problem-solving skills

There is no question that a key source of trouble in small group activities is the unevenness of skill levels among participants. If the group leaders have skills, both the leaders and some of the members will be able to devise steps for goal achievement or game plans to eliminate the causes of problems. It will also be possible to begin implementing those plans. When problems occur during the implementation process, however, the skills of group leaders will not be enough to guarantee success. If there is too much dependence on group leaders at this point, members will lose their sense of belonging to the group and the activities will fail.

It is therefore essential to nurture problem-solving skills. This is generally the reason for instituting self-improvement techniques such as independent study groups. It is not always easy, however, to link theory with practice.

In the past, small group activities were exclusively a priority of secondary industries. By 1975, however, interest in such activities had extended to tertiary industries. If the small group activities at retail and other tertiary industries take on purposes of improving business results, there is a danger that those activities will become too remote from daily work.

Similarly, a too-strong focus on problems directly related to daily work activities will cause psychological resistance among worksite members. Trying to have it both ways is probably characteristic of Japan.

In tertiary industries, where women do so much of the work, small group activities will be strongly affected by the workers' attitudes toward labor and the job. It will probably be difficult to get their cooperation when the activities are held outside regular working hours. Moreover, when there is a lot of movement of workers in and out of worksites, small group activities become increasingly superficial and less efficient. For this reason, tertiary industries should make it a policy to have regular members at the worksite.

Small group activities in Japan mean future progress

The future of small group activities in Japan will be determined by changes expected to occur in the country's industrial structure and management environment. Specifically, the following patterns are predicted.

1. Problem-solving activities will become increasingly related to goal-oriented management, dealing with management goals, worksite goals, and topics that involve related problems.
2. Activities that improve group solidarity will become more important as a means to increase efficiency.

3. There will be an increasing tendency to promote self-improvement through education groups and on-the-job training.
4. Problem-solving activities will become the most common type of small group activities. The key to their progress will be the development of cooperating structures with future personnel.

The more small group activities come to emphasize goals and results, the more management systems for the lower levels of company organization will become a problem. This is why: When small group activities attach importance to results and to improvement of those results, workers become more interested in their own normal work activities. This increases their consciousness of the worksite management system, which is likely to result in a problem of participation in decision making by worksite regular employees.

One of the characteristics of Japanese small group activities is their basis in the idea that progress depends on satisfaction of members' individual desires and aspirations as well as satisfaction of their need to make a contribution to the company. This will continue to characterize small group activity in the future. The apparent contradiction here is something that companies will be coping with as they acquire new business. Another problem that will become common to all small group activities will be that of organizing things according to a single format and at the same time creating multiple energy sources.

7

Skills Map for Organizers with Vision

Two Managers

Visionary Director of a Branch Store: The Case of Teraoka

Business section chief Teraoka of a medium-size business machine marketing company was transferred to a certain branch store. This store was on old territory, and its sales figures were sluggish. Even though there were many new sales personnel among the sales section chiefs, the SE technicians were too few, making full development of new areas impossible. However, the company had expanded with a new factory, and the market situation could not be considered in any sense to be bad. Instead, it seemed that the troubles with SE and business concerning due dates stemmed from store management being pressed by short-term transactions.

After observing for a while, Teraoka made a proposal. "Why don't we think about what we'd like this branch store to be three years from now? At the very least, shouldn't we double current sales in the next three years?"

Almost everyone opposed this. "We're already working as hard as we can this month," they said. "We don't have time to dream." The implication was that Teraoka was a dreamer.

But Teraoka refused to give up. He summoned people besides those in leadership and held an overnight meeting. There he reviewed current conditions and described trends for the next three years in the business machine industry. He warned that if nothing were done now, in three years the branch store would be virtually unable to respond to needs and would thus be facing bankruptcy.

So began the vision management of the branch store. People began generating ideas for the three-year goals and ways to achieve

149

those goals. For the younger employees, it was the first time that ideas about the store had been consistent.

Subsequently, whenever people came up with reasons for not being able to do something, Teraoka encouraged them to look for what was *possible*, not for what was *impossible*. Instead of focusing on reasons that had been relevant in the past, he urged employees to consider the conditions that would make something possible, then work to create those conditions. It was his belief that change occurs in small steps and that success would come if employees tackled each step one at a time.

Analysis of Actual Conditions and Sound Planning: The Case of Saeki

Branch store manager Saeki was feeling burdened by the goal of a 20 percent increase for the current year, a goal that had been set at a conference of branch store managers. In the two years he had managed the store, there had never been such an increase in performance set.

The store was located in a city whose commercialism was solidly established. Although there had been no great development, the city offered stability. The twelve employees at the store were also dependable. Many were from the local area, and they could be described as steady, industrious types.

To achieve the goal of a 20 percent increase, Saeki ordered a reexamination of current and prospective customers. Judgments were made about the number of current users who might switch to new types of machines, particularly to product X, and about the results of product expansion.

The following week, together with business section chiefs and persons in charge of operations, Saeki went over each person's report and established total figures. The figures looked unrealistic, but Saeki hoped that an increase in legwork would bring them into reach.

At the same business conference in which goals for branch managers had been set, emphasis was placed on development in the city's western districts. Three-month plans were clarified and a blueprint was submitted. Conference leaders requested that a goal attainment progress report be submitted weekly at the business conference, and that the number of visits be further increased. From his own experiences, Saeki had developed a philosophy that a steady advance in business came from trust and legwork rather than from theories.

Skills Required of Administrators

The purpose in describing these two cases is not to consider the strengths and weaknesses of the administrators, but rather to show how the two men used their differing abilities. Each responded to the goal in a different but skillfully organized way.

The abilities required of administrators are listed according to a system devised by specialists to evaluate administrative abilities (see Figure 7-1). The number of items, even in Japan, easily exceeds 70 to 80. The abilities relevant here, however, can be arranged along the following two axes.

- *Vertical Axis:* The power to step into an unknown world and solidify your present position (in management terms, attack and defense). Also, the power to fix attention on the future while maintaining the present.
- *Horizontal Axis:* The power to make the best use of your own and others' strengths.

The resulting quadrants indicate the four administrator types. They may be labeled in the following way:

1. The *creative development manager*, who cuts a path into the future by making the best use of others (manager)
2. The *creative development specialist*, who cuts a path into the future by relying on his or her own abilities (inventor)
3. The *problem-solving manager*, who maintains the present by making the best use of others (master builder)
4. The *problem-solving specialist* who maintains the present by relying on his or her own abilities (craftsperson)

The question might be asked, Shouldn't a manager be either a type 1 or a type 3? The answer is no. Disallowing the use of individual abilities will make it difficult to ascertain the immediate future, to maintain the present without making blunders, and to involve others. Similarly, by limiting managers to types 2 and 4, a

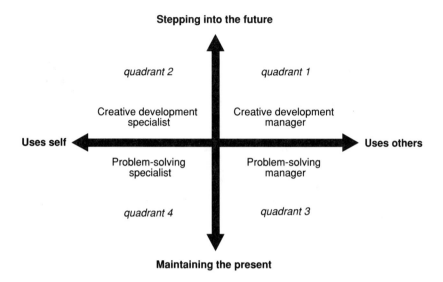

Figure 7-1. Abilities of Administrators

company risks losing the involvement of other employees. The ideal manager seeks to involve others in a process whereby his or her own strengths are linked to the end result.

If these categories are applied to the case studies just discussed, then branch manager Teraoka is the creative development type of manager, and Saeki is the problem-solving type of manager. However, their abilities extend into quadrants 2 and 4 also.

This diagram is most useful as a tool for clarifying your own abilities and for indicating areas that need further development. In addition, keep in mind that the diagram represents not just administrative abilities but also abilities required of an "organization person" (manager).

Requirements of a Manager

Four Basic Abilities

There are four basic abilities required of an organization person, each corresponding to one of the quadrants represented in Figure 7-2.

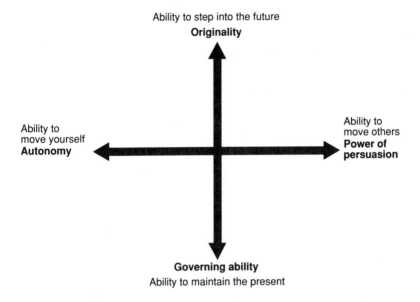

Ability to step into the future
Originality

Ability to
move yourself
Autonomy

Ability to
move others
**Power of
persuasion**

Governing ability
Ability to maintain the present

Figure 7-2. Primary Requirements of an Organization Person

Ability to step into the future (originality)

No one can truly see into the future. But perhaps a more important skill is the willingness to create a vision of the future, a vision unencumbered by past experience and preconceived ideas. What is essential, in other words, is originality.

Ability to sustain the present (governing ability)

Sustaining the present, in management terms, is "defense." This consists of governing current actions according to already known standards. In other words, your output reflects your understanding of the rules and customs for work and the expectations of superiors, top executives, and customers.

Ability to motivate others (power of persuasion)

The ability to motivate others is the ability to convey your intentions to others in such a way that they adopt the same intentions. In other words, it is the power to persuade. This is one characteristic of leadership. Talking down to a person in a forcible, coercive manner might also be called persuasion. But the quality sought in an organization person is of a subtler yet stronger nature: It gets other people to agree with your aims, adopt them as their own, and then work for them on their own. Furthermore, it gets them to feel growth in the process.

The ability to motivate yourself (autonomy)

To improve your abilities and put them to work, you need above all a positive attitude. This both motivates you to develop your abilities and gives you the self-confidence to work toward your goals without being swayed by others.

Ways to Strengthen Managerial Abilities

Ability to step into the future. Beyond developing a concept not tied to past experience, you need to refine the concept as your own idea and explicitly offer it as a vision. Otherwise, you will be nothing more than the "possessor of a unique idea."

Ability to sustain the present. Beyond handling a given condition with certainty, you must indicate concretely what you are aiming at and construct a program for attaining it. Otherwise, you will be a person who acts only according to the letter, not the spirit.

Ability to motivate others. Beyond being able to persuade individuals, you must also be able to pull a group toward your goal, gaining both the consent and the cooperation of each member involved. Otherwise, you will be unable to move the organization as a whole.

Ability to motivate yourself. If you set out to accomplish only what you are responsible for, you will become isolated in self-satisfied complacency. However, if you look beyond those responsibilities into the essence of the work, you will be able to use personnel and information to their best advantage. Then your problem-solving actions become both efficient and effective.

Figure 7-3 shows the requisite abilities for an organization person. Although these abilities are not confined to management, they are grouped under the general category of administrative characteristics. As seen in the cases of Teraoka and Saeki, these characteristics are the prime determinants of success in management.

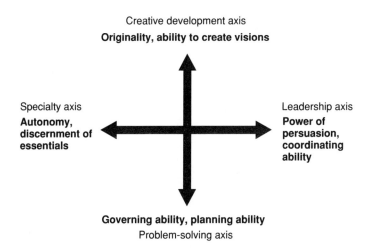

Figure 7-3. Secondary Requirements of an Organization Person

Action Characteristics that Support Administrative Characteristics

Several of the administrative characteristics just described assume a partnership between individuals and groups. Such a partnership demands that the characteristic of one party be demonstrable to the other party. For example, the ability to persuade will be weakened by a perceived lack of strength and perseverance or a perceived failure to engage in decisive words and conduct. In other words, the administrator's qualities must both exist and be fully evident to other workers.

Consequently, three additional characteristics are needed: vitality (strength), tenacity (perseverance), and risk-taking (mental strength). These are called action characteristics (see Figure 7-4).

Action characteristics do not simply qualify the skills of administrators. They also determine the degree to which administrators can influence others.

Using Maps to Grasp Ability Tendencies

When administrative characteristics are shown in matrix form, as in Figure 7-4, the area of each quadrant changes by the strength

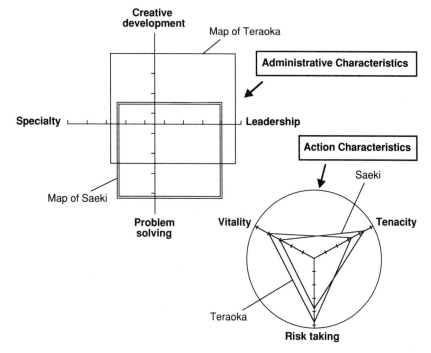

Figure 7-4. Ability Map of Organization Person

of abilities for the respective axes. This "ability map" graphically depicts a manager's organizational skills and tendencies. The action characteristics appear in the triangular portion of the fan-shaped matrix. Such a format shows at a glance which abilities managers should develop.

Relationship between Axes, Abilities, and Action Characteristics

To read an ability map, you need to understand the relationship between the four axes, eleven abilities, and three action characteristics. A detailed explanation of this relationship follows.

Creativity development: the ability to innovate

As mentioned, it is not enough to handle adroitly the problems you have been assigned. Effective managers will have ideas for the future concerning their own duties and workplace. They will be able to step into the unknown and aim for a "fluctuation" by which something new can be created.

This field of ability can be subdivided as follows.

The ability to create visions. The ability to create requires a strong personal viewpoint, a clear picture of the future and of the means to get there, and a multifaceted perspective.

If you were asked to describe what your job and activities would be like in one, two, or three years from now, would you be able to give a clear answer? Every person who manages an organization has a vision — either conscious or subconscious — of the working conditions he or she would like to create. The problem is to put that vision in precise form. That should not be someone else's work. Furthermore, along with a clear articulation of vision should come a program for implementation, so that the vision becomes reality. *The capacity to describe an attractive future and the path to it is the ability to create visions.* That ability reveals itself in

- the articulation of a personal vision so that it becomes a collective vision
- the articulation of a vision that is a leap forward rather than merely a measure to improve current conditions
- a policy that includes a listing of specific obstacles expected during implementation of that policy
- a policy that includes alternate proposals of means to achieve it

Originality. If the ability to create visions is the capacity to formulate both an ideal and the means to attain it, then the person creating the visions must be able to follow through with originality — the ability to conceive ideas not bound to conventional perspectives. These novel perspectives — the ones considered to be impossible or too fantastic to take seriously — are indispensable to innovation. Originality reveals itself in

- opinions and plans that are completely different from those of others
- a dislike of routine ways of doing things
- a tendency to come up with ideas when others have none

- the ability to translate the seemingly impossible into reality through systematic action

Problem solving: the ability to understand a task and handle it with efficiency

The ability to solve problems is a characteristic of able managers. When people with this ability are handed assignments, they know how to skillfully maneuver within the given conditions and with given resources to steadily achieve their ends. They react to any problems encountered not by devising original solutions but by attending to the short-term future and controlling conditions. Problem solvers are very powerful within the organization.

Planning ability. Planning ability can be subdivided into two general abilities. One is the ability to put into clear and concrete form *either as quantitative or qualitative goals* those assignments and goals handed down by top echelons or other departments.

The second is the ability to prepare precise procedures for reaching these goals. A plan of action is not some vague outline whose outcome is unclear. Rather, it is a carefully constructed schedule in which due consideration has been given to the level of urgency, degree of importance, and potential problems involved, and which can be faithfully implemented. It should be flexible, including alternate plans to be used in the event that the original plan becomes unfeasible. It includes no waste or unreasonable steps and makes efficient use of time.

Governing ability. Governing ability is the ability to cope with deviations from standards in a clear-cut manner through a process of problem solving. It enables you to stick to a plan as the norm for action and implementation. That requires a tenacious and resolute stance toward goal attainment. Underlying this ability is constant vigilance and assessment of work progress as well as an understanding of the relationship between actual circumstances and the goal. Moreover, you must be willing to take immediate action to correct or eliminate any discrepancies discovered. You must be almost compulsive about keeping work on schedule and pinpointing the source of obstacles to that schedule. Indifference has no part in governing ability. By contrast, the following traits are consistent with this ability.

- Interest in the work methods and progress of subordinates
- Dissatisfaction with any situation that has not reached its goal level
- Uneasiness when subordinates do not report
- Strict adherence to due dates
- Insistence on standards that are consistent
- If something is no good, a willingness to say so

Leadership

Leadership is the ability to move individuals and groups in the direction of organizational goals. It is the ability to use others to produce results rather than to rely solely on yourself. The "others" you are involved with are not merely your subordinates. Because today's complex problems are rarely confined to a single workplace, a more cooperative, interdepartmental approach is required. Consequently, you should be able to extend your influence to colleagues and superiors as well as to subordinates. Certainly leadership strongly depends on the personality of the leader and on the appropriateness of the course chosen. Its essential ingredient, however, is the ability to motivate others. This in turn requires the power of persuasion and coordinating ability.

Power of persuasion. The power of persuasion is a fundamental component of leadership ability. It is not enough to merely put others to work. More important is whether their work is fueled by an understanding of your intentions. Conveying your intentions in such a way that they become others' intentions as well allows you to draw upon positive qualities in others and make the best use of their skills. Without such an understanding, they will work at only half their capacity.

The power to persuade is particularly important in your relations with colleagues and superiors, when you lack the advantage afforded by a position of authority. But no matter whom you are dealing with, your aim is the same: to motivate others through an appeal to their hearts and minds. In doing so you must be able to express with certainty your aims in a way that is clear to others. You also need to present in suitable terms the bases and necessity of those aims, based on objective information. Finally, you need to be receptive to other viewpoints so that you can respond to any doubts expressed. The following behaviors are indicative of the power to persuade.

- You are firmly committed to a course of action that is unrelated to your own interests.
- You convey both your point and the rationale for that point clearly and logically.
- You present your case from a variety of perspectives while trying to forge a thoroughgoing mutual agreement.
- You clearly explain the result desired and the conditions for its attainment.
- You put forward your ideas without undue concern over their reception.

Coordinating ability. Coordinating ability is the ability to build a system in which there are common goals and objectives. It is based on a thorough understanding of ideas held in common and on the ability to keep groups of people functioning as cohesive units. Specifically, the following traits are indicative of coordinating ability.

- You facilitate mutual understanding of ideas and the differences between them by eliciting and confirming the views of all concerned.
- You accurately read the feelings of individuals and groups and know who needs to be persuaded.
- You are not distracted by a multiplicity of viewpoints from your intention to arrive at a solid conclusion based on reality and the true substance of the matter.
- You turn a scene of emotional discord into a positive experience by clarifying the points at issue and then presenting a path for discussion.
- When talks are deadlocked around superficial matters, you resolutely step in to end the impasse.

Specialization

Specialization is the ability to specify a problem, understand its true nature and causes, and solve it through your own ability. It is not always necessary and indispensable for leaders themselves to have the problem-solving abilities. Rather, the ability to motivate people who have such abilities is the essential quality of leadership. By contrast, specialization requires you to employ your own skills in identifying and solving problems. The image here is of a specialist or craftsperson.

The ability to discern the essence of things. The ability to get to the heart of a mass of information is basic to specialization. You are able to discern the essence of things when

- you can accurately identify the focal point during technology development
- you can precisely indicate the core problems affecting your section
- you correctly understand the causes of mechanical breakdowns
- you know what to say in order to win over a customer

The question is whether you can traverse the shortest distance to a problem solution, as in these cases. When a problem appears, you do not respond in some arbitrary fashion. Rather, you firmly grasp the root cause of the problem and then devise measures accordingly.

Autonomy. Autonomy is the ability to think and act without being influenced by others. It enables you to strongly defend your own position within the organization. As a first-rate specialist, you note the trends and ideas around you without straying from your own basic ideas and values. You have the self-confidence to take your views to their logical conclusion, even if it means putting yourself at risk. You are not autonomous if you change your opinions after listening to others, or depend on texts and mentors for guidance on actions. On the other hand, you do have autonomy if

- you remain unswayed by others' views and actions
- you are not satisfied with anything unless you have initiated it and carried it out yourself
- you remain undaunted by opposition

Even small concessions are inconsistent with autonomy when they compromise strong convictions.

Action power

Action power is the willingness and ability to exercise your intrinsic abilities. Your abilities will be useless to the organization if they remain dormant. Self-development through the acquisition of new skills and knowledge is a worthy activity as long as it results in something more than a sense of self-satisfaction. To wield action power, you must commit your abilities to action. For this you need the three essential elements of vitality, risk taking, and tenacity.

Vitality. Vitality is the force that enables you to present yourself in a positive way and to take actions that overflow with energy, regardless of the situation or the assignment.

Activeness, defiance, initiative, and energy are some of the general terms for vitality. Especially needed today are the strength of body and character to move ahead despite numerous obstacles. Some of the signposts of vitality are

- an eagerness to try things
- a willingness to take risks
- a dislike of losing to others
- a high level of energy and drive
- strength of word and deed
- perseverance
- a tendency to embrace challenge rather than compromise your course of action
- a tendency to view setbacks as opportunities to improve ability

Risk taking. Taking a risk means asserting your position in the face of uncertain conditions and impending difficulties.

Recently, there has been a tremendous increase in the number of risk-filled and unpopular decisions being made. Prolonging current actions is easy, but it is not the course for a person who will move the organization. Decision making requires firm resolve and a willingness to take responsibility for results. You are able to take risks when

- you rely on your judgment to formulate proposals and then clearly articulate them to others despite anticipated criticism
- you insist on testing an action by trying it out
- you stick to your convictions even when ambiguities arise

- you opt for bold measures carrying heavy responsibility over limited measures for which you will not be held accountable
- you are willing to make a final decision when others cannot do so

Tenacity. Tenacity is the ability to see through to the end either an assigned duty or your own decision. You cannot lead others if you are too ready to abandon set goals or measures that prove difficult or appear to be of limited value.

In this age of innovation, you need to actively adopt challenging new approaches. However, no matter how brilliant the approach, if it is pursued only half way it will bring no results. Difficulties go hand in hand with innovation. You need to explore all avenues of a given approach before giving up on it. You show tenacity when

- you see a job through to its completion
- you persevere despite repeated failure and without despairing
- you work at a steady pace despite numerous distractions
- you maintain efforts to reach a goal during the assigned time period even if that goal has become less desirable during the process of its achievement
- you persist in trying to obtain agreement on a point even if the other party is not listening

Assessing Your Own Abilities

You can assess your own abilities through use of the checklist provided in Figure 7-5. Score your abilities as follows:

5 Extremely strong tendency
4 Fairly strong tendency
3 Cannot say either way
2 Not much of a tendency
1 Almost no tendency at all

Next, take the average point score for each ability and obtain the total points for each axis. Transfer these numbers to the blank

Administrative Characteristics		Insufficient				Sufficient
A. **Creative** **Development**	**1. Ability to create visions** • You have your own image of what your job will be like in the future, based on internal and external changes. • Instead of analyzing current levels of dissatisfaction, you prefer to think about future possibilities • You relate your ideas about the future to superiors and subordinates and zealously engage in discussion.	Average point score ☐ 1 2 3 4 5 1 2 3 4 5 1 2 3 4 5				
	2. Originality • Instead of following conventional frameworks and common knowledge, you advance through your own methods and ways of thinking. • You are able to draft proposals that use 3 or 4 methods instead of just 1. • You come up with ideas even when others have none.	Average point score ☐ 1 2 3 4 5 1 2 3 4 5 1 2 3 4 5				
B. **Problem** **solving**	**3. Planning ability** • You never start work until the desired result has been made clear. • You establish a clear order of priorities and move forward accordingly. • You make careful preparations and are not flustered by small problems.	Average point score ☐ 1 2 3 4 5 1 2 3 4 5 1 2 3 4 5				
	4. Governing ability • You maintain customs and rules, and see that others follow them. • When there is a divergence from goals, you do not hesitate to institute corrective measures. • Once a time limit has been set, you follow it, even if it is mistaken.	Average point score ☐ 1 2 3 4 5 1 2 3 4 5 1 2 3 4 5				
C. **Leadership**	**5. Power of persuasion** • For the most part others look favorably on your views and work along the lines of your intentions. • Instead of insisting on one view, you assert your position on the basis of an understanding of others' thoughts and feelings. • Despite opposition, you say what needs to be said without hesitation.	Average point score ☐ 1 2 3 4 5 1 2 3 4 5 1 2 3 4 5				
	6. Coordinating Ability • When opposing views create confusion at the workplace, you get both sides to listen to reason and make adjustments. • You handle things by understanding the ideas and feelings of each person, and the power relationships among them. • When discussion reaches a deadlock, you are able to suggest a way out that everyone can agree to begin taking action on.	Average point score ☐ 1 2 3 4 5 1 2 3 4 5 1 2 3 4 5				

Figure 7-5. Ability Assessment Checklist

Administrative Characteristics	Insufficient		Sufficient
D. Specialization / **7. Ability to Discern Essentials** • You grasp the true causes behind current problems and take measures against those causes. • You consider your own work problems from a broad perspective. • You can look at current conditions in the workplace and state explicitly what the priority problems are; in addition you have ideas concerning them.	Average point score □ 1 2 3 4 5 1 2 3 4 5 1 2 3 4 5		
8. Autonomy • You use your own judgment even when others do not agree with you. • You make all decisions yourself and are not satisfied unless you do things yourself. • You prefer to work with subordinates who have individual outlooks and behavior rather than with those who simply cooperate.	Average point score □ 1 2 3 4 5 1 2 3 4 5 1 2 3 4 5		

E. Action characteristics	Insufficient		Sufficient
9. Vitality • Confronted by a host of problems, you resolutely solve them one by one. • You are not satisfied with current conditions and demand more challenging goals of both yourself and others. • Having asserted your views, you work tirelessly on their behalf.	Average point score □ 1 2 3 4 5 1 2 3 4 5 1 2 3 4 5		
10. Risk taking • You use your judgment to make decisions even when uncertain about the results. • You act according to your beliefs despite criticism from others. • You move boldly ahead even when the path is ill-defined.	Average point score □ 1 2 3 4 5 1 2 3 4 5 1 2 3 4 5		
11. Tenacity • You refuse to give up on a course of action until results are reached that can be agreed upon. • You sustain an approach until all methods have been exhausted. • The fluctuating feelings of the moment do not sway you from your path.	Average point score □ 1 2 3 4 5 1 2 3 4 5 1 2 3 4 5		

spaces on the map. After becoming familiar with the examples in Figure 7-5, try to draw the ability map shown in Figure 7-6. Then refer to the descriptions that follow.

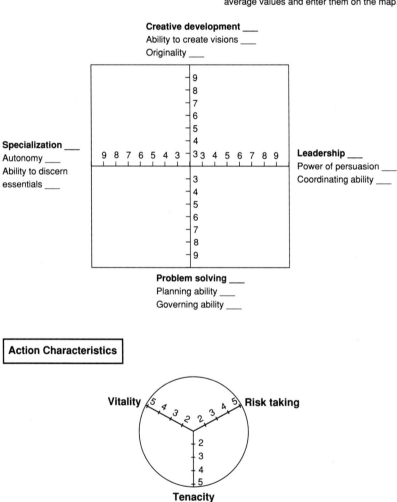

Figure 7-6. Your Ability Map

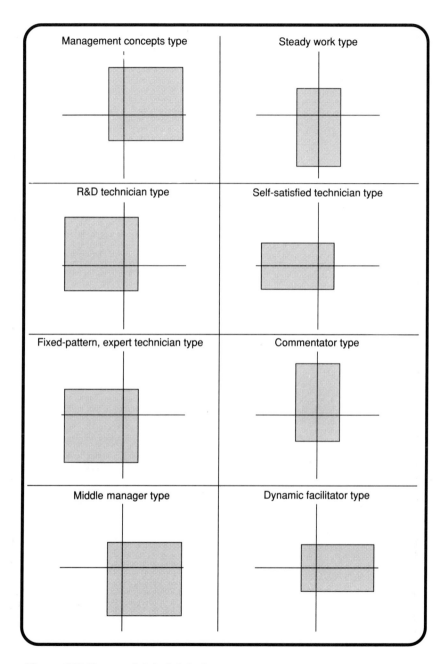

Figure 7-7. Types of Administrators

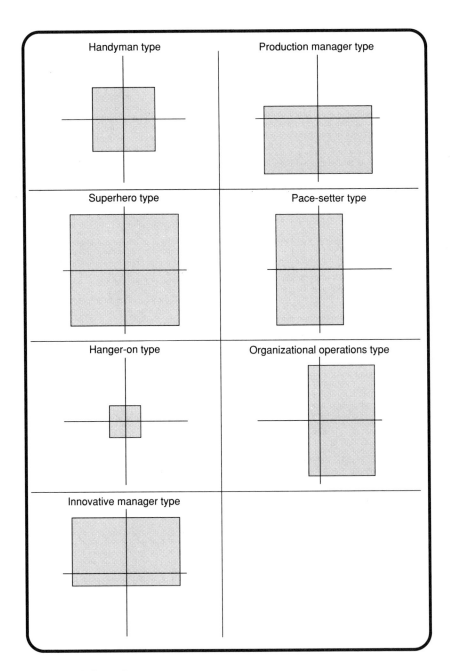

Figure 7-7. (cont.)

Types of Administrators

Once you have completed the ability map, match the results against those in Figure 7-7, to gain an idea of what type of administrator you are. Descriptions of the fifteen types identified follow.

Management Concepts Type. You bring a managerial perspective to all aspects of your job. You regularly study and are sensitive to world trends. Rather than seclude yourself, you actively engage in your work, present your views to others, and make your influence felt. However, you sometimes become estranged from the 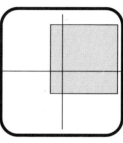 grind of everyday reality. You should be wary of becoming labeled as a commentator or of engaging in flattery of superiors.

R&D Technician Type. A research and development technician or a planning development worker occupies an important position that influences the direction of the company as a whole. From the broadest perspective, these people create problems to develop improvement conditions. With a tenacious focus on a single point, they are 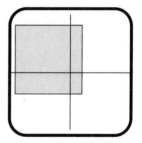 continually engaged in generating ideas. Because of this, the specific results of your efforts are not always visible. This tendency will be less pronounced if you reduce the distance between worksite and market and focus on ideas that are directly related to company needs.

Fixed-pattern, Expert Technician Type. Whatever the assignment, you carry it through to completion without deviating from your course. Within the organization you are known as a trustworthy, reliable, and responsible person. On the negative side, your limited scope of skills becomes a liability when cooperation with 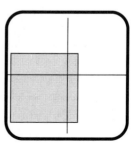 others is needed. Because you are apt to be somewhat stiff and awkward in personal relations, you do not always make your contribution to the organization known to others.

Middle Manager Type. Making good use of past experience, you receive assignments with confidence and maintain a steady worksite operation.

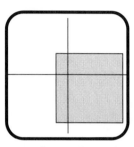

You pay close attention to performance at the worksite and to human relations, and you compare well with others in attaining immediate goals. However, your perspective on future goals and improvement goals tends to be deficient.

Steady Work Type. You are the veteran of the organization, having been long rooted in your workplace. You have an image as a reserved craftsperson. You complete your assignments reliably, working at a pace that is steady yet comfortable. However, your subordinates do not develop under you, and you rarely become involved in groups,

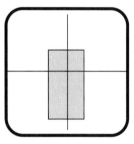

as you prefer to do everything yourself. You need to broaden your scope of human relations and teach your skills to others by delegating more work to subordinates.

Self-Satisfied Technician Type. Your scope of interests and concerns is narrow. You are capable of sustaining a concentrated effort on one problem and are highly knowledgeable in one area. On the reverse side, you are totally immersed in your own world, are apt to resent intervention by others, and are often stubborn and inflexible in

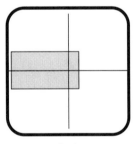

your personal relations. You view things in terms of victory or defeat, black and white. You need to develop greater regard for the views of others.

Commentator Type. You have a strong viewpoint that is strongly colored by study. Your pronouncements have a theoretical air, and you are articulate in your delivery. You often make proposals that will permit some situation to be exploited. Your image is that of a veritable person of action. However, your tendencies to leave things 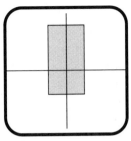 undone and not go beyond mere words cost you the confidence of your own people and hamper real progress. You need to build up slow but steady efforts in the daily work routine.

Dynamic Facilitator Type. Confronted with a problem, you immediately seize the initiative, asserting your own ideas, motivating the group, and performing your own duties with zeal. You excel in so-called personal skills. Very often, you are a standout in the group as a coordinator.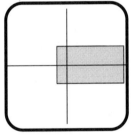

Because you are so ready to step into any situation, you may be trampling over other peoples' ideas or rushing to action before the goal is sufficiently understood. You need to take more time to assess the situation before leaping into it.

Handyman Type. You respond faultlessly to every administrative situation but without any individuality. In terms of personality characteristics, you are tractable and easily influenced by others. You fit into any situation and do not go against the tide. You have an image as a not-always-reliable fix-it person. You probably need to 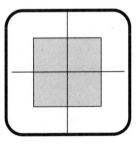 stake out a position that will clarify your goals.

Superhero Type. You take stock of yourself and your goal-oriented self-study efforts in a straightforward manner. You are possessed of a character of great scope that gives thought even to growth in personal relations. You will almost certainly join the managerial elite in the future. You are a person of talent capable of developing on

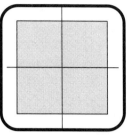

your own. In short, you are a "superhero." The downside of this is the possibility that your very excellence will inhibit the growth of your successor. You need to temper your abilities with a reserved stance that allows others to develop.

Hanger-On Type. In a situation where self-preservation is the goal, instead of pushing your ideas and actions to the foreground, you bury yourself in everyday work. You are a person of limited talents, passing time quietly.

Although you faithfully follow directions, your performance fails to meet the

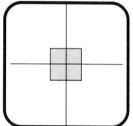

expectations of your superiors. As a result, your status in the organization declines further each year. You need to improve your situation by developing one area of strength.

Innovative Manager Type. You are sensitive to trends of the times. You are always coming up with original concepts. You put in enough legwork on your concepts to make them a reality. You inject vitality into the organization.

On the negative side, your concepts are sometimes too advanced, eccentric, or

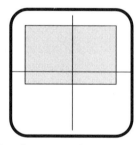

ill-defined for the organization to pursue. So that you don't risk becoming known as a person of showy or shallow ideas, you need to pay more attention to solid perspectives that are based on an understanding of current conditions.

Production Manager Type. You are a parent figure, a boss type who knows every aspect of your workplace, has a high degree of personal expertise, and also has your subordinates well in hand. Your superiors rest easy when you are entrusted with something, and subordinates also have confidence in you. However, your perceived 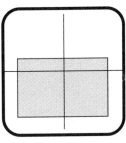 usefulness to the organization is limited to situations in which past experience is applicable. If there are changes in the environment or in past ways of doing things, this limitation reveals itself. You need the modesty that comes with dissatisfaction over the current state of affairs, a broad perspective on the business and its future, and contemplation of various courses of action.

Pace-setter Type. You excel in all areas, with keen intuition and insight as your weapons. You exhibit superior foresight, and your work is flawless. On the negative side, you love splendid isolation. You do not rely on others, and your egotistical, go-it-alone style antagonizes those around you.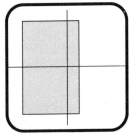

As an administrator you ignore subordinates and assume all of the work. Consequently, your subordinates are unable to develop their skills. You need to take an interest in training the next generation of workers and in cooperating with people who have abilities that you lack.

Organizational Operations Type. As a manager, you are constantly trying to improve results and solidify future prospects. You have the ability to establish an energetic workplace. However, you use little of your own thinking or work. Rather, you skillfully handle the talented persons around you. This leaves you pow- 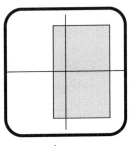 erless when the organization is limited to new employees or to employees with similar abilities. You need to improve your own judgment abilities and rely more heavily on those.

Leaders for the Coming Era

In a recent survey conducted by Sangyo Noritsu University, subordinate section chiefs were asked what they considered most important in the actions of their general managers. The most common answers were the following:

- They should have concrete strategies to support the realization of visions.
- They should have a voice and influence with top management.
- They should properly allocate management resources for the implementation of plans.

The first answer refers to creativity, the second to leadership, and the third to problem solving. To restate the general theme of this book, the ability to both offer a vision and give it concrete form is the basis of leadership. To realize that, you must be able to manage people and abilities, things and money — and thus be able to influence those at the top.

Conversely, things not expected of divisional general managers were concentrated in the following areas:

- Explicit demonstrations of behavioral standards expected of subordinates
- Harsh demands for goal attainment
- Changing the organization and plans to fit the situation

The results of this survey show that the old carrot-and-stick approach to quantitative goals is no longer appropriate. Innovation does not appear on demand; nor does it emerge from a stubborn reliance on past experience. Rather, it requires the vision of a leader and the mutual understanding and assent of subordinates.

Take another look at your own map. Think about the direction you want your organization to move in, and the kind of leader that will be required to move it. If you compare your current abilities with those that will be required two or three years from now, it should become clear what areas you need to develop and what areas you should make use of now.

8

Need for a New Perspective

Over the last ten years or so, we have been involved in education and consulting work for numerous companies. We have found that most companies still lack the managerial and administrative know-how and technology needed to deal with fundamental problems. This may be attributable to insufficient study and research on the part of managers and administrators, as well as consultants and researchers. Whatever the reason, it is a problem that will not be easily solved.

First of all, the changes companies are experiencing today are not like a smoothly ascending slope, where past ways of doing things retain some validity. Rather, they are like a staircase whose risers leap beyond reach of existing know-how and technology. When companies encounter such "risers," it is time to innovate and achieve qualitative growth. What is required of managers and administrators is not the upgrading and implementation of already existing know-how and technology but the motivating force that gives subordinates the courage to step out into the dark. In effect, they become *agitators* — or perhaps *prophets* is a better term. Either term suggests the seminal role that managers play during periods of extreme changes.

This book has been written to help the reader understand such periods. It is based on the belief that you *can* acquire the know-how and technology needed for scaling those "risers," as well as the courage to step out into an uncertain future. Specifically, it offers the following five basic concepts.

Paradigm Change

The concept of paradigm is difficult to explain, but it can be understood here as the conscious and subconscious conceptual frameworks and generally accepted ideas of a particular group.

A paradigm is shaped by society and shared experiences, so that it becomes almost an article of faith. But although it is unquestioned by the group that has created it, its meaning will be lost on another society with different experiences — and different paradigms. Thus, a paradigm is meaningful only so long as the history and experiences that produced it are still relevant — to return to the stair analogy, only when times are poised on a "tread." When companies come up against a riser, however, old paradigms are no longer effective and must be discarded.

To throw away a paradigm is nothing more than to throw away a temporal creation whose relevance is purely relative. Initially, it may be unsettling to deny deeply ingrained convictions and assumptions. But in the final analysis, there is perhaps no position less secure than one based on convictions and assumptions that no longer bear any relation to reality.

Action-Research

Action-research is the attitude to assume when stepping into the future. As mentioned in Chapter 2, this involves going through the following steps.

Step 1: Taking experimental actions based on various hypotheses under circumstances of considerable stress and uncertainty

Step 2: Reconstructing hypotheses after gathering information and data on original hypotheses and interpreting their significance

Step 3: Taking additional experimental actions based on new hypotheses

These steps involve continuous daily efforts.

Generally speaking, the reverse approach, research-action, is considered to be the "scientific approach" to the future.

Thorough collection and analysis of information on present and projected situations are performed, after which decisions are made about future behavior.

The difference between the two approaches is this: The research-action approach uses data collection and analysis to look into the future; using this approach is like trying to shoot an arrow into the center of a target. By contrast, the action-research approach is used to get a macroview of the distance to the target and the size of the target itself.

The research-action approach tries to achieve a perfect score with a single "shot," while the action-research approach aims at a perfect score that results from a series of various processes. To use another analogy, the action-research approach is like a ship that sends out intermittent radio waves to detect schools of fish.

The research-action approach uses existing data to achieve solid control over the future, while the action-research approach uses unfolding data to clarify and thus control actual situations.

A more fundamental difference between these two approaches is the following. The research-action approach is based on the idea that there exist in society invisible rails to direct us. That is, there are always "correct" solutions to problems; success depends on getting a clear understanding of what they are. The action-research approach, on the other hand, is based on the idea that there are no rails in society. Rather, rails are forged as a result of actions over time. That is, the solution will vary according to the time elapsed and the results of various actions; therefore, success depends on clearly understanding the results of actions (reactions) and on acting more quickly.

Some of the reasons for proposing an action-research approach are explained in Chapter 2. Now let's consider some other reasons from a different perspective.

Taking action when you have little prospect of success is extremely unnerving. To allay your anxiety, therefore, you focus on the collection and analysis of information, in the hope of improving your chance for success. This approach, research-action, is effective during times of gradual change (when society rests on the "tread" of the time "staircase"). That is because it is possible to make relatively accurate estimates about the future by studying existing data.

But when times are changing rapidly (are in their "riser" mode), the use of existing data is an ineffective means of understanding the overall picture or of making estimates about the future.

Although the attempt to improve future prospects by gathering and analyzing data is considered to be analysis for management, it is actually analysis for the sake of analysis. That is, when dramatic changes occur, and a research-action approach is used, it becomes necessary to devote an enormous amount of time and energy to research for clarifying the actual situation. Moreover, once that research is completed, the actual situation has changed again. As noted in Chapter 2, no matter how much time and energy are invested, it is impossible to anticipate everything when dealing with a social phenomenon like that of company management.

An even more troubling problem is the delay in deciding what direction to take caused by the lengthy process of research. This prevents other employees from taking action and causes them to resent and distrust management.

Sticking to the research-action approach during times of dramatic change is like standing at the golfing tee making interminable calculations before hitting the ball. Certainly, the drive from the tee is important, but subsequent shots to regain position are also important. To hit your objective, you must first believe that you can hit it and then make bold efforts to do so. The action-research approach must of course not be a simple brutal act. Rather, it is a process carried out with an independent sense of responsibility and mission.

Vision Approach

To assume another perspective, there are two ways of approaching the future. One of these emphasizes process; the other emphasizes vision.

The process approach is focused on the present. That is, it interprets the present as a product of the past and the future as something resulting from the present. The assumption is that a concentration of energy on the present will guarantee stability and profit in the future.

By contrast, the vision approach is focused on the future. It begins with the question, What do we want to become? On the basis of the answer, a strategy for the present is formulated. The present is thus interpreted as a means to realize the future.

The effectiveness of the process approach is limited, not because it lacks an image of the future but because it is based on a false image of the future — as something that flows logically from the present. By contrast, the vision approach is based on the assumption that the future results from your own independent intentions. That is, the future is what you choose it to be. Therefore, it is important to envision a future that is in accordance with your own beliefs. By doing that, you make it possible to blaze a trail through uncertain conditions.

The Importance of Top Management

When faced with an uncertain future, companies generally rely on two so-called scientific methods of making decisions. The first method is based on the collection and analysis of information, while the second method is based on discussion and consensus.

The problem with these methods is that they both presuppose a future determined by past experiences. The data analyzed in the first method is the product of past conditions, as are the judgments made in the second method. Thus the bases of these methods become irrelevant during times of critical changes.

At such junctures (when companies come to a "riser") you need to move beyond "scientific" methods to the hands-on method of learning by doing. This lessens the possibility of making mistaken judgments based on irrelevant data or self-interest.

If management does not succeed when carried out "scientifically," then neither does it succeed when based on the consensus of those "being managed." The independent will of the manager is always essential to successful management.

The move in many companies from *omikoshi* or bottom-up management, to leader-oriented, top-down management is indicative of this. The companies that prosper throughout tumultuous times will be led by those who make decisions based on their own responsibilities and their own intentions.

Innovations in the Basic Structure of Management

There are two main types of management innovation approaches that companies should use in responding to changes in the environment. One of them is innovation at the level of the basic management structure. This means making innovations in things such as concept construction, strategy planning, branch companies, mergers and acquisitions, and division integration, as well as making innovations in the basic characteristics and skeletal structure of the management system. The other type of innovation is carried out at the level of the organization administration system. This means making innovations in methods to achieve goals such as operations systems, work content, work allocation, problem treatment and solution methods, systems, procedures, and skills.

The first type of innovation involves changes in resource allocation itself or in basic ideas about the distribution of management resources. The second type, however, involves changes in methods of utilizing resources that have already been distributed. Generally speaking, the former type requires decisions at major management levels, while the latter type requires decisions at the level of worksite activities.

In the past, Japanese companies have tended to favor the latter type of approach — innovation at the level of the organization administration system. TQC, QC circles, robots, mechanization, and computer systems are all products of that approach. Such innovations are intended to maximize efficiency.

Although this type of innovation continues to be used today, an increasing number of companies are also making innovations in the basic management structure. It is against this backdrop that this book was conceived.

Making innovations at the level of basic management structure is a creative response to rapid changes in the environment. Even if such changes bring no immediate response, they may still bring success in the future or, at the very least, stave off the trouble that would result from leaving the old management system intact. Such an extended sphere of influence is absent from innovation at the organization administration level.

Management is a complex social phenomenon, given to many areas of gray and few areas of black or white. Successful managers will be able to steer a course through gray areas and eras of change. The authors of this book have outlined a system for doing so — broadly called vision management but incorporating the many concepts described above — in the hope that readers will understand it and benefit from it.

BOOKS AVAILABLE FROM PRODUCTIVITY PRESS

Productivity Press publishes and distributes materials on continuous improvement in productivity, quality, customer service, and the creative involvement of all employees. Many of our products are direct source materials from Japan that have been translated into English for the first time and are available exclusively from Productivity. Supplemental products and services include newsletters, conferences, seminars, in-house training and consulting, audio-visual training programs, and industrial study missions. Call 1-800-274-9911 for our free book catalog.

Technoshifts
Meeting the Challenge of Technological Change
Smail Ait-El-Hajd

Technoshifts presents a broad perspective of the phenomenon of ongoing technological advancement and the corporate mentality and organization necessary to respond to it most effectively. More than a theoretical discussion, this book examines the recent shift in industrial, mechanical, and electromechanical technologies. This concrete analysis helps you recognize the indicators of future shifts and use new technologies to the utmost advantage. It also describes steps you can take to respond rapidly to the threats and opportunities of the current technological environment.
ISBN 0-915299-83-6 / [224 pages] / $34.95 / Order code TECHNO-BK

Hoshin Kanri
Policy Deployment for Successful TQM
Yoji Akao (ed.)

Hoshin kanri, the Japanese term for policy deployment, is an approach to strategic planning and quality improvement that has become a pillar of Total Quality Management for a growing number of U.S. firms. This book is a compilation of examples of policy deployment that demonstrates how company vision is converted into individual responsibility. It includes practical guidelines, 150 charts and diagrams, and five case studies that illustrate the procedures of hoshin kanri. The six steps to advanced process planning are reviewed and include a five-year vision, one-year plan, deployment to departments, execution, monthly audit, and annual audit.
ISBN 0-915299-57-7 / [256 pages] / $49.95 / Order code HOSHIN-BK

Championship Management
An Action Model for High Performance
James A. Belohlav

Many current books extol the values of being an excellent company. This book goes beyond that to explain how excellence can be achieved and why it is so critically important. A model for action demonstrates how any company can become a "championship" caliber company. Further, it explains why some excellent companies lose their edge while others remain excellent, and why still others appear to be excellent but are not.
ISBN 0-915299-76-3 / 272 pages / $29.95 / Order code CHAMPS-BK

Productivity Measurement Handbook
William F. Christopher

A compilation of practical, detailed methods for measuring productivity company-wide that has become a standard reference book. Measurement makes productivity performance visible and provides a feedback system that helps everyone do a better job. This book explains standard economic formulas and includes query forms for assessing measurement, case studies, charts for overhead projection, and an extensive bibliography.
ISBN 0-915299-05-4 / 680 pages / 3-ring binder / $137.95 / Order code PMH-BK

The Service Era
Leadership in a Global Environment
Franco D'Egidio

Through anecdotes, case studies, and the presentation of a clear and straightforward business philosophy, this book examines the crisis of current Western business strategy in its lack of a service-oriented perspective. D'Egidio challenges management to develop both strategy and corporate culture based on the critical "moment of truth" for any business: the point of contact with the customer. After supporting the claim that quality service is more important than quality products, the book offers eight strategic directions for dealing with the challenge of competition based on a global service orientation.
ISBN 0-915299-68-2 / 184 pages / $29.95 / Order code SERA-BK

Today and Tomorrow
Henry Ford

The inspiration for Just-In-Time. Originally published in 1926, this autobiography by the world's most famous automaker has been long out of print. Yet Ford's ideas have never stopped having an impact, and this book provides direct access to the thinking that changed industry forever. Here is the man who doubled wages, cut the price of a car in half, and produced over 2 million units a year. Time has not diminished the progressiveness of his business philosophy, or his profound influence on worldwide industry. You will be enlightened by what you read, and intrigued by the words of this colorful andremarkable man.

ISBN 0-915299-36-4 / 286 pages / $24.95 / Order code FORD-BK

Winning Ways
Achieving Zero-Defect Service
Jacques Horovitz

Building a quality service program is essential these days, especially when you consider the high cost of low quality service. This book teaches the service manager how to launch a quality service program and covers techniques for measuring and delivering high standard quality service, ways to detect and eliminate errors, and methods for measuring customer satisfaction. With self-diagnostic questions at the end of each chapter, this simple but thorough how-to book will inspire and lead you to improved customer service performance.

ISBN 0-915299-78-X / 176 pages / $24.95 / Order code WWAYS-BK

Tough Words for American Industry
Hajime Karatsu

Let's stop "Japan bashing" and take a good close look at ourselves instead! Here is an analysis of the friction caused by recent trade imbalances between the United States and Japan — from the Japanese point of view. Written by one of Japan's most respected economic spokesmen, this insightful and provocative book outlines the problems and the solutions that Karatsu thinks the U.S. should consider as we face the critical challenge of our economic future. For anyone involved in manufacturing or interested in economic policy, this is a rare opportunity to find out what "the other side" thinks.

ISBN 0-915299-25-9 / 190 pages / $24.95 / Order code TOUGH-BK

Measuring, Managing, and Maximizing Performance

Will Kaydos

You do not need to be an exceptionally skilled technician or inspirational leader to improve your company's quality and productivity. In non-technical, jargon-free, practical terms this book details the entire process of improving performance, from "why" and "how" the improvement process works to "what" must be done to begin and to sustain continuous improvement of performance. Special emphasis is given to the role that performance measurement plays in identifying problems and opportunities.

ISBN 0-915299-98-4 / 304 pages / $34.95 / Order MMMP-BK

Inside Corporate Japan
The Art of Fumble-Free Management

David J. Lu

A major advance in the effort to increase our understanding of Japan, this book shows why Japanese businesses are run as they are—and how American companies can put this knowledge to good use. Lu has spent many years in Japan, personally knows many top leaders in industry and government, and writes with a unique bicultural perspective. His very readable book is full of anecdotes, case studies, interviews, and careful scholarship. He paints a well-rounded picture of the underlying dynamics of successful Japanese companies. *Inside Corporate Japan* is a timely and invaluable addition to your library.

ISBN 0-915299-16-X / 278 pages / $24.95 / Order code ICJ-BK

Performance Measurement for World Class Manufacturing
A Model for American Companies

Brian H. Maskell

If your company is adopting world class manufacturing techniques, you'll need new methods of performance measurement to control production variables. In practical terms, this book describes the new methods of performance measurement and how they are used in a changing environment. For manufacturing managers as well as cost accountants, it provides a theoretical foundation of these innovative methods supported by extensive practical examples. The book specifically addresses performance measures for delivery, process time, production flexibility, quality, and finance.

ISBN 0-915299-99-2 / [448] pages / $49.95 / Order code PERFM-BK

Productivity Press, Inc., Dept. BK, P.O. Box 3007, Cambridge, MA 02140 1-800-274-9911

COMPLETE LIST OF TITLES FROM PRODUCTIVITY PRESS

Akao, Yoji (ed.). **Quality Function Deployment: Integrating Customer Requirements into Product Design**
ISBN 0-915299-41-0 / 1990 / 387 pages / $ 75.00 / order code QFD

Akiyama, Kaneo. **Function Analysis: Systematic Improvement of Quality and Performance**
ISBN 0-915299-81-X / 1991 / 288 pages / $59.95 / order code FA

Asaka, Tetsuichi and Kazuo Ozeki (eds.). **Handbook of Quality Tools: The Japanese Approach**
ISBN 0-915299-45-3 / 1990 / 336 pages / $59.95 / order code HQT

Belohlav, James A. **Championship Management: An Action Model for High Performance**
ISBN 0-915299-76-3 / 1990 / 265 pages / $29.95 / order code CHAMPS

Birkholz, Charles and Jim Villella. **The Battle to Stay Competitive: Changing the Traditional Workplace**
ISBN 0-915-299-96-8 / 1991 / 110 pages / $9.95 /order code BATTLE

Christopher, William F. **Productivity Measurement Handbook**
ISBN 0-915299-05-4 / 1985 / 680 pages / $137.95 / order code PMH

D'Egidio, Franco. **The Service Era: Leadership in a Global Environment**
ISBN 0-915299-68-2 / 1990 / 165 pages / $29.95 / order code SERA

Ford, Henry. **Today and Tomorrow**
ISBN 0-915299-36-4 / 1988 / 286 pages / $24.95 / order code FORD

Fukuda, Ryuji. **CEDAC: A Tool for Continuous Systematic Improvement**
ISBN 0-915299-26-7 / 1990 / 144 pages / $49.95 / order code CEDAC

Fukuda, Ryuji. **Managerial Engineering: Techniques for Improving Quality and Productivity in the Workplace** (rev.)
ISBN 0-915299-09-7 / 1986 / 208 pages / $39.95 / order code ME

Gotoh, Fumio. **Equipment Planning for TPM: Maintenance Prevention Design**
ISBN 0-915299-77-1 / 1991 / 320 pages / $75.00 / order code ETPM

Grief, Michel. **The Visual Factory: Building Participation Through Shared Information**
ISBN 0-915299-67-4 / 1991 / 320 pages / $49.95 / order code VFAC

Hatakeyama, Yoshio. **Manager Revolution! A Guide to Survival in Today's Changing Workplace**
ISBN 0-915299-10-0 / 1986 / 208 pages / $24.95 / order code MREV

Hirano, Hiroyuki. **JIT Factory Revolution: A Pictorial Guide to Factory Design of the Future**
ISBN 0-915299-44-5 / 1989 / 227 pages / $49.95 / order code JITFAC

Hirano, Hiroyuki. **JIT Implementation Manual: The Complete Guide to Just-In-Time Manufacturing**
ISBN 0-915299-66-6 / 1990 / 1006 pages / $2500.00 / order code HIRANO

Horovitz, Jacques. **Winning Ways: Achieving Zero-Defect Service**
ISBN 0-915299-78-X / 1990 / 165 pages / $24.95 / order code WWAYS

Ishiwata, Junichi. **I.E. for the Shop Floor 1: Productivity Through Process Analysis**
ISBN 0-915299-82-8 / 1991 / 208 pages / $39.95 / order code SHOPF1

Japan Human Relations Association (ed.). **The Idea Book: Improvement Through TEI (Total Employee Involvement)**
ISBN 0-915299-22-4 / 1988 / 232 pages / $49.95 / order code IDEA

Productivity Press, Inc., Dept. BK, P.O. Box 3007, Cambridge, MA 02140 1-800-274-9911

Japan Human Relations Association (ed.). **The Service Industry Idea Book: Employee Involvement in Retail and Office Improvement**
ISBN 0-915299-65-8 / 1991 / 294 pages / $49.95 / order code SIDEA

Japan Management Association (ed.). **Kanban and Just-In-Time at Toyota: Management Begins at the Workplace** (rev.), Translated by David J. Lu
ISBN 0-915299-48-8 / 1989 / 224 pages / $36.50 / order code KAN

Japan Management Association and Constance E. Dyer. **The Canon Production System: Creative Involvement of the Total Workforce**
ISBN 0-915299-06-2 / 1987 / 251 pages / $36.95 / order code CAN

Jones, Karen (ed.). **The Best of TEI: Current Perspectives on Total Employee Involvement**
ISBN 0-915299-63-1 / 1989 / 502 pages / $175.00 / order code TEI

JUSE. **TQC Solutions: The 14-Step Process**
ISBN 0-915299-79-8 / 1991 / 416 pages / 2 volumes / $120.00 / order code TQCS

Kanatsu, Takashi. **TQC for Accounting: A New Role in Companywide Improvement**
ISBN 0-915299-73-9 / 1991 / 244 pages / $45.00 / order code TQCA

Karatsu, Hajime. **Tough Words For American Industry**
ISBN 0-915299-25-9 / 1988 / 178 pages / $24.95 / order code TOUGH

Karatsu, Hajime. **TQC Wisdom of Japan: Managing for Total Quality Control**, Translated by David J. Lu
ISBN 0-915299-18-6 / 1988 / 136 pages / $34.95 / order code WISD

Kato, Kenichiro. **I.E. for the Shop FLoor 2: Productivity Through Motion Study**
ISBN 1-56327-000-5 / 1991 / 224 pages / $39.95 / order code SHOPF2

Kaydos, Will. **Measuring, Managing, and Maximizing Performance**
ISBN 0-915299-98-4 / 1991 / 304 pages / $34.95 / order code MMMP

Kobayashi, Iwao. **20 Keys to Workplace Improvement**
ISBN 0-915299-61-5 / 1990 / 264 pages / $34.95 / order code 20KEYS

Lu, David J. **Inside Corporate Japan: The Art of Fumble-Free Management**
ISBN 0-915299-16-X / 1987 / 278 pages / $24.95 / order code ICJ

Maskell, Brain H. **Performance Measurement for World Class Manufacturing: A Model for American Companies**
ISBN 0-915299-99-2 / 1991 / 448 pages / $49.95 / order code PERFM

Merli, Giorgio. **Total Manufacturing Management: Production Organization for the 1990s**
ISBN 0-915299-58-5 / 1990 / 304 pages / $39.95 / order code TMM

Mizuno, Shigeru (ed.). **Management for Quality Improvement: The 7 New QC Tools**
ISBN 0-915299-29-1 / 1988 / 324 pages / $59.95 / order code 7QC

Monden, Yasuhiro and Michiharu Sakurai (eds.). **Japanese Management Accounting: A World Class Approach to Profit Management**
ISBN 0-915299-50-X / 1990 / 568 pages / $59.95 / order code JMACT

Nachi-Fujikoshi (ed.). **Training for TPM: A Manufacturing Success Story**
ISBN 0-915299-34-8 / 1990 / 272 pages / $59.95 / order code CTPM

Nakajima, Seiichi. **Introduction to TPM: Total Productive Maintenance**
ISBN 0-915299-23-2 / 1988 / 149 pages / $45.00 / order code ITPM

Nakajima, Seiichi. **TPM Development Program: Implementing Total Productive Maintenance**
ISBN 0-915299-37-2 / 1989 / 428 pages / $85.00 / order code DTPM

Productivity Press, Inc., Dept. BK, P.O. Box 3007, Cambridge, MA 02140 1-800-274-9911

Nikkan Kogyo Shimbun, Ltd./Factory Magazine (ed.). **Poka-yoke: Improving Product Quality by Preventing Defects**
ISBN 0-915299-31-3 / 1989 / 288 pages / $59.95 / order code IPOKA

Nikkan Kogyo Shimbun/Esme McTighe (ed.). **Factory Management Notebook Series: Mixed Model Production**
ISBN 0-915299-97-6 / 1991 / 184 pages / $175.00 / order code N1-MM

Nikkan Kogyo Shimbun/Esme McTighe (ed.). **Factory Management Notebook Series: Visual Control Systems**
ISBN 0-915299-54-2 / 1991 / 194 pages / $175.00 / order code N1-VCS

Nikkan Kogyo Shimbun/Esme McTighe (ed.). **Factory Management Notebook Series: Autonomation/ Automation**
ISBN 0-56327-002-1 / 1991 / 200 pages / $175.00 / order code N1-AA

Ohno, Taiichi. **Toyota Production System: Beyond Large-scale Production**
ISBN 0-915299-14-3 / 1988 / 162 pages / $39.95 / order code OTPS

Ohno, Taiichi. **Workplace Management**
ISBN 0-915299-19-4 / 1988 / 165 pages / $34.95 / order code WPM

Ohno, Taiichi and Setsuo Mito. **Just-In-Time for Today and Tomorrow**
ISBN 0-915299-20-8 / 1988 / 208 pages / $34.95 / order code OMJIT

Perigord, Michel. **Achieving Total Quality Management: A Program for Action**
ISBN 0-915299-60-7 / 1991 / 384 pages / $45.00 / order code ACHTQM

Psarouthakis, John. **Better Makes Us Best**
ISBN 0-915299-56-9 / 1989 / 112 pages / $16.95 / order code BMUB

Robinson, Alan. **Continuous Improvement in Operations: A Systematic Approach to Waste Reduction**
ISBN 0-915299-51-8 / 1991 / 416 pages / $34.95 / order code ROB2-C

Robson, Ross (ed.). **The Quality and Productivity Equation: American Corporate Strategies for the 1990s**
ISBN 0-915299-71-2 / 1990 / 558 pages / $29.95 / order code QPE

Shetty, Y.K and Vernon M. Buehler (eds.). **Competing Through Productivity and Quality**
ISBN 0-915299-43-7 / 1989 / 576 pages / $39.95 / order code COMP

Shingo, Shigeo. **Non-Stock Production: The Shingo System for Continuous Improvement**
ISBN 0-915299-30-5 / 1988 / 480 pages / $75.00 / order code NON

Shingo, Shigeo. **A Revolution In Manufacturing: The SMED System**, Translated by Andrew P. Dillon
ISBN 0-915299-03-8 / 1985 / 383 pages / $70.00 / order code SMED

Shingo, Shigeo. **The Sayings of Shigeo Shingo: Key Strategies for Plant Improvement**, Translated by Andrew P. Dillon
ISBN 0-915299-15-1 / 1987 / 208 pages / $39.95 / order code SAY

Shingo, Shigeo. **A Study of the Toyota Production System from an Industrial Engineering Viewpoint** (rev.)
ISBN 0-915299-17-8 / 1989 / 293 pages / $39.95 / order code STREV

Shingo, Shigeo. **Zero Quality Control: Source Inspection and the Poka-yoke System**, Translated by Andrew P. Dillon
ISBN 0-915299-07-0 / 1986 / 328 pages / $70.00 / order code ZQC

Shinohara, Isao (ed.). **New Production System: JIT Crossing Industry Boundaries**
ISBN 0-915299-21-6 / 1988 / 224 pages / $34.95 / order code NPS

Sugiyama, Tomo. **The Improvement Book: Creating the Problem-Free Workplace**
ISBN 0-915299-47-X / 1989 / 236 pages / $49.95 / order code IB

Suzue, Toshio and Akira Kohdate. **Variety Reduction Program (VRP): A Production Strategy for Product Diversification**
ISBN 0-915299-32-1 / 1990 / 164 pages / $59.95 / order code VRP

Tateisi, Kazuma. **The Eternal Venture Spirit: An Executive's Practical Philosophy**
ISBN 0-915299-55-0 / 1989 / 208 pages/ $19.95 / order code EVS

Yasuda, Yuzo. **40 Years, 20 Million Ideas: The Toyota Suggestion System**
ISBN 0-915299-74-7 / 1991 / 210 pages / $39.95 / order code 4020

Audio-Visual Programs

Japan Management Association. **Total Productive Maintenance: Maximizing Productivity and Quality**
ISBN 0-915299-46-1 / 167 slides / 1989 / $749.00 / order code STPM
ISBN 0-915299-49-6 / 2 videos / 1989 / $749.00 / order code VTPM

Shingo, Shigeo. **The SMED System**, Translated by Andrew P. Dillon
ISBN 0-915299-11-9 / 181 slides / 1986 / $749.00 / order code S5
ISBN 0-915299-27-5 / 2 videos / 1987 / $749.00 / order code V5

Shingo, Shigeo. **The Poka-yoke System**, Translated by Andrew P. Dillon
ISBN 0-915299-13-5 / 235 slides / 1987 / $749.00 / order code S6
ISBN 0-915299-28-3 / 2 videos / 1987 / $749.00 / order code V6

Returns of AV programs willl be accepted for incorrect or damaged shipments only.

TO ORDER: Write, phone, or fax Productivity Press, Dept. BK, P.O. Box 3007, Cambridge, MA 02140, phone 1-800-274-9911, fax 617-864-6286. Send check or charge to your credit card (American Express, Visa, MasterCard accepted).

U.S. ORDERS: Add $5 shipping for first book, $2 each additional for UPS surface delivery. CT residents add 8% and MA residents 5% sales tax. For each AV program that you order, add $5 for programs with 1 or 2 tapes, and $12 for programs with 3 or more tapes.

INTERNATIONAL ORDERS: Write, phone, or fax for quote and indicate shipping method desired. Pre-payment in U.S. dollars must accompany your order (checks must be drawn on U.S. banks). When quote is returned with payment, your order will be shipped promptly by the method requested.

NOTE: Prices subject to change without notice.